W9-BGR-786

...NTRY & MACHINE GUN SUMMER COURS...

A SOLDIER'S

THE PERSONAL PHOTOGRAPHS OF CANADIANS AT WAR 1939–1945

VIEW

BLAKE HEATHCOTE

DOUBLEDAY CANADA

Endpaper: The Royal Canadian School of Infantry, Machine Gun Summer Course, Niagara-on-the-Lake, 1937. i: A sign inside the German border. These were the last days of the war, but there were still renegade SS and Hitler Jugend to deal with who would fight until their last breath. ii: Doug Appleton on guard duty at the Trenton Air Base. October 1940. iii: Harold Ridley having a bath the only way possible in the desert at Quayara, Iraq. iv: Winter at sea. v: Jean-Claude Dubuc with fellow Fusiliers Mont-Royal in front of Notre Dame, Paris, 1945. vi: A Canadian grave at Hill 72, Tilly-la-Campagne (Verrières Ridge), August 1944. vii: A starving Dutch boy on the streets of Amsterdam, shortly after liberation. viii–ix: A church in Normandy, 1944.

Copyright © 2005 Blake Heathcote

All rights reserved. The use of any part of this publication, reproduced, transmitted in any form or by any means electronic, mechanical, photocopying, recording or otherwise, or stored in a retrieval system without the prior written consent of the publisher—or, in the case of photocopying or other reprographic copying, a license from the Canadian Copyright Licensing Agency—is an infringement of the copyright law.

Doubleday Canada and colophon are trademarks.

LIBRARY AND ARCHIVES CANADA CATALOGUING IN PUBLICATION
Heathcote, Blake
   A soldier's view : the personal photographs of Canadians at war, 1939-1945 / Blake Heathcote.
ISBN 0-385-66000-6
1. World War, 1939-1945—Pictorial works. 2. World War, 1939-1945—Canada—Pictorial works. I. Title.
D768.15.H395 2005   940.53'022'2   C2005-904031-9

Printed and bound in Canada

Published in Canada by Doubleday Canada, a division of Random House of Canada Limited

Visit Random House of Canada Limited's website: www.randomhouse.ca

TRANS 10 9 8 7 6 5 4 3 2 1

For our parents and their grandchildren. We will not forget.

—Blake Heathcote

May 1, 1944, off Portsmouth, England. For several days, sailors onboard HMCS *Prince David* watched exercises such as this with a Landing Craft Assault, and thought that this was "IT", but it turned out just to be a dress rehearsal. These soldiers would not be standing easy if it were the real thing.

CONTENTS

Dick Likely on a route march at OTC, Brockville, Ontario, in the summer of 1941.

I recommend this remarkable book of photographs of Canada's part in the Second World War. I became a war artist in that war and made some drawings and paintings; at the same time I realized that many people, both professionals in film and photo units, and amateurs, were making records by photography.

A few years ago I met Blake Heathcote, the creator of this collection and the grandson of Major Eric Heathcote who administered the war artists' part of the Historical Section of the Canadian Army. Of course I knew Eric Heathcote—for a brief time at the end of the war we roomed in the same house in Chelsea in London. Blake had an intense interest in World War II as a result of his closeness to his grandfather, and edited a book of interviews with veterans. This collection of photographs and brief captions, collected from many sources, has a kaleidoscopic nature: the very randomness of images from the three services, taken in many different places and over the nearly six years of the war, seems to give a truer sense of the chaos of war than a more systematic selection and grouping would.

I admit to being puzzled by the present interest in the events of more than sixty years ago, but if you are interested this book will absorb you.

Alex Colville
Nova Scotia, June 2005

INTRODUCTION

I remember lying on the floor of my grandfather's study poring over a scrapbook of his photos from the war. I was perhaps ten or eleven years old, and this was something new to me. My grandfather was, in equal parts, a soldier and an artist. On the walls of his house hung many of his watercolours from the war years and, in a place of pride, his formal officer's portrait painted in London during the war. There were also studio photographs of him in uniform taken in London, where he'd been second in command to C.P. Stacey of the Historical Unit of the Canadian Army.

But this scrapbook was something different; as it turned out, it was also something I wasn't supposed to be looking at. Some time later, I asked my father about the scrapbook and he suggested that I not mention it to Grandpa, as it was something quite personal of his. So I kept it to myself, but I kept it.

It turns out that Eric, my grandfather, was writing his memoirs of his three years in the trenches in the Great War, with the Toronto Scottish during the 1930s, and of his time in London during World War II. Being a "picture man," he had begun laying out his story using sketches he'd done and photos he'd accumulated over the years. What I'd seen was an artist's sketchbook of his life, his way of marking moments he didn't want to forget. He never managed to write more than a few pages, beautifully hand-lettered on massive folio sheets. I didn't see his scrapbook again for another thirty years, ten years after he'd died and twenty years after he'd stopped working on it, lost in Alzheimer's.

Corporal Eric Heathcote (right) on leave in Belgium, spring 1917.

The scrapbook was, in many ways, the tip of the iceberg. Dad discovered a cache of contact sheets and negatives in my grandfather's army trunk, a transportable wardrobe complete with drawers and hangers and countless compartments that held everything an officer might choose to carry with him.

The photos that Dad found were tucked in beside Eric's five-year wartime diary and a handful of crowns, shillings and thrupenny bits. These images were less about his life and more about the people whose lives were so deeply scarred by the war. I don't think he knew what to do with them—they were difficult to look at—but he kept them nonetheless.

I have since discovered from many veterans that the heart of their wartime lives was often reflected in the photos they took. Not everyone had a camera, but those who did weren't reluctant to share them. Sometimes the photos I was shown were stored in shoeboxes, and other times kept in places of pride. Even when the photos spoke of times and places that veterans did not care to remember in too much detail, the pictures were kept as an irrefutable, irreplaceable link to their past. The secret to discovering this past is that you have to ask.

Looking at veterans' photos in the company of those who took them is a deeply meaningful experience. When the photos are spread out before them, memories spring to life, returning veterans to what many refer to as "the best years of my life." On page 107 of *A Soldier's View* there is a photo of a gang of Typhoon pilots horsing around between ops. These guys flew tough low-level missions against German ground troops; they were a major factor in the Allies' success at Falaise in 1944. The mood of this picture seems wildly at odds with the danger of their work. There is a sad irony here too: a few weeks after it was taken most of the pilots in the picture had been killed. It was taken by Alex Gray, whose photographic duties with the RCAF included recording operational squadrons, the aircraft they flew, and the wreckages of planes that crashed. His photos span the lives and deaths of these men, and in recounting his experiences with both, a hardness comes into his voice, common to those vets who were witness to the extremes of life on the front lines.

When it came to choosing what photographs to include in this book, I resorted to the simple method of taking ones that elicited the most powerful memories from their owners, thereby generating insight into how war is experienced first-hand.

I've come to appreciate that what matters most about a photograph is the emotion it inspires. Great pictures don't answer our questions; they show us why questions should be asked. However wrenching an image may be, its deepest power lies in opening the viewer up to something that extends past the boundaries of time and history to reveal events on an individual and human scale.

Percy Loosemoore, a few months too young to enlist in World War I, joined up at the beginning of the next war as a mature man in his forties. He served for six years overseas with the Royal Canadian Army Pay Corps. This branch of service, like all supply units, was never far behind the front line. As the Canadian Army moved from an offensive role to one of occupation, the RCAPC provided service to our soldiers throughout Europe. In this capacity, Percy had the unique opportunity to travel extensively, on the heels of battle and through the wake of the war's destruction in villages and towns across the Continent. Being a noncombatant afforded him the chance to use his camera, and he diligently photographed most everything he saw. When he returned to Canada in 1946, he spent the next seven years feverishly recording what he'd seen and experienced during those years and meticulously cataloguing his photographs.

He was sad to have missed much of his children's formative years while he was away, but he had no regrets. In 1946, he wrote, "I feel conscious of fulfilling a duty, [and] of a pride in the knowledge that I have contributed part of my life to what I believed to be a great cause. It is somewhat consoling to know you have not lived completely in vain, and that you have been part . . . of a great human struggle to better the world for future generations."

He died in 1953, a few months after completing his work of wartime remembrance. His album of photographs, which is one of the finest I've ever seen, seems to have been an encompassing purpose in life in those few years after the war. I believe that he hoped his children and grandchildren might see it as a means of understanding something of his experience that he himself was unable to come fully to terms with.

Looking at his pictures, particularly those taken in the spring and summer of 1945, and reading his notes about them, I think that Percy was looking to find some solace amidst the unfathomable destruction. He seems to have found hope for the future and delight in the resilience of youth in the smiles and colourful dresses of the young German schoolgirls he noticed while passing through a small village, their hesitant and shy faces full of curiosity and innocence.

All veterans want what Percy wanted: for their contribution in the war to be acknowledged as part of something greater than themselves.

The photographs in *A Soldier's View* are of a generation at war, and they preserve a chain of experience that words can't always convey. I'm sure that's why they were taken and why they have survived from generation to generation.

From their photographs, I have come to know my father's and grandfather's worlds as seen through their eyes. The meaning of these pictures and stories deepens with the passage of time and keeps these memories very much alive today.

Jean-Claude Dubuc of Les Fusiliers Mont-Royal enjoying the simple pleasures in Trafalgar Square in the summer of 1944, shortly before embarking for the Continent.

ON THE ROAD

Men of the 1st Canadian Parachute Battalion around noon on April 30, 1945, crossing the Elbe River on a pontoon bridge. This was a very effective method of quickly erecting a river crossing, but spacing and the balance of weight had to be carefully monitored.

World War II was not a Canadian war, but a war in which Canada fought. It's an important distinction when you consider just how small our country, let alone our armed forces, were at the end of the 1930s.

There were around five thousand people on active service when Canada declared war in September 1939 for the first and only time in its history. And yet, by 1945, over a million Canadians had seen service—almost ten percent of the population.

There were many reasons for enlisting in those years, and as I look at the enthusiastic, young faces in these pictures, it seems obvious that adventure was high on the list. This generation had grown up in the shadow of the Great War, yet the romance of going to war was still reason enough to sign up. As he prepared to disembark from his landing craft, Lou Pantaleo (Royal Regiment of Canada) remembers thinking, "You knew you weren't gonna get hurt. You know, all the movies and everything else, the good guys always win." And then Lou's unit landed at Puys as part of the Dieppe raid in 1942, and the war changed hard and fast.

The immediacy and sweep of war are meaningful only to someone who's been there, and those who found themselves in the thick of it encountered sights for which they could never have been prepared.

The understanding that the veterans came to of what the war was about was usually limited to what they personally saw and experienced. As I began to work on my archive of veterans' photographs and stories, I realized that the individual perspective that each person had was, for me, the most vivid and moving way to understand what war must have been like.

Almost every veteran I met couldn't wait to get into the fight, and that eagerness is what I see in the photos in this section. They joined up because they wanted more out of life—and to hell with the cost. On the road to war, they had to overcome every conceivable hardship and obstacle. With every new challenge, those young men and women found their way to a richer sense of what it means to be alive.

These are photographs of Canadians on a road that would ultimately give them more than they were looking for and that would forever change the way they saw the world.

Above: New Women's Royal Canadian Naval Service (WRCNS or "Wrens") recruits collect their naval code books at Ste-Hyacinthe, Quebec, their signals training centre during the war, 1944. The Navy was the last branch of the Canadian armed forces to accept women recruits, but it ultimately afforded the quickest route into active service. Women were paid one third of what men earned, and there was discrimination, both from within military ranks and from the wider community. The Wrens persevered, however, and by the war's end there were more than six thousand in service.

Opposite: My father, E.B. Heathcote, age 19, shortly after enlisting in the army against his father's wishes. My grandfather, who served in both wars, did not want his son to follow suit. Although Dad managed to join, he found himself trapped at Vimy Barracks in Kingston for the duration. In 1970, my grandfather confessed that one of his close friends was Commandant at Vimy, and that through this man's good graces, he had prevented Dad from getting overseas.

Above: Christmas 1939 on Yorke Island, taken at night by the light of a Coleman gas lamp in the 1st HQ hut, 15th Field Artillery Regiment, RCA. The island was a small, isolated outpost, and the gunners' uniforms suggest how dated the entire post was. Left: August 29, 1939, on board the Canadian minesweeper HMCS *Comox* headed for Yorke Island, where there was a battery to protect the northern entrance to the inland waters off Vancouver. By the 1930s, Japan had become an aggressively expansionist power. The threat of an attack by Japanese armed merchant vessels and submarines was serious. Gun batteries would enforce security regulations and protect the air station, moored vessels and port facilities.

Wally Loucks, RCAF WAG (wireless air gunner) in the tedious but familiar job of guard duty. One of the first stages in most servicemen's basic training, it was a pedestrian albeit effective means of buckling a new recruit down to the brass tacks of military life. Wally recalls that the gun was nearly as tall as he was. One of the great tricks young recruits learned was how to fall asleep while standing guard; it's harder than it sounds.

The faces of enthusiastic, young recruits. Clockwise from top left: Tom Ingham, stoker on HMCS *Iroquois*; Marcel Croteau, DFC, air gunner; Art Wallace (left) and two shipmates on shore leave; Leopold Beauchamp (left) and a fellow trooper from the famed Van Doos (Royal 22nd Regiment); renowned paratrooper Tommy Prince (right) and his brother, Maurice, both extraordinary soldiers; 14-year-old seaman cadet Alex Jardine; and Jim Jamieson, air crew, killed on a bombing run over Europe, one of many lost in the war.

Above: Outside the crew room at No. 1 ETFS (Elementary Training Flying School) Malton, Ontario, in January 1941. Pictured are Hay Clarke, Wynn Brewer, Doug Campbell, Clarke Adams, and "Turk" Bayly. They wear the heavy insulated coveralls, boots and helmets of aircrew. This wardrobe was a far cry from the silk scarves and goggles that many had envisioned when they'd first signed up, but it kept them warm in unpressurized aircraft flying at twenty thousand feet.

Opposite, top left: O.J. "Dusty" Lutes in Brandon, Manitoba, 1942. Top, right: Navigator/Bomb Aimer in training Doug Appleton at Malton, Ontario, 1941. Bottom: RCAF-WD (Women's Division) in Labrador, winter 1944. This entertainment unit travelled North America and overseas, performing their show *All Clear* for Allied troops. Many men serving on bases in Labrador hadn't seen a woman for years.

Below: Dale Brecknell (third from right) and other members of the DR (dispatch riders) graduating class in Kingston during the summer of 1942. DRs were essential to front-line fighting, and they suffered an unusually high casualty rate. In convoying men and machinery, the DRs had to ride up and down the line with orders and information, often at night without lights. A lone rider on a Norton was a vulnerable target for other speeding vehicles. On the front lines, DRs were often prime targets for snipers, as they were unable to return fire. But those who loved the big bikes loved the job.

Opposite: Victor Wong (right) and two fellow troopers at a SOE Force 136 training camp in Chilliwack, British Columbia, 1944. Chinese Canadians were considered British subjects and not accorded any of the benefits of Canadian citizenship, although many were second- and third-generation Canadians. An overwhelming number volunteered for SOE (Special Operations Executive) service in Burma and China. They were trained to fight in the jungles of Pacific Rim countries controlled by the Japanese. The elite members were parachuted behind enemy lines to work with local guerrilla forces.

Trixie (Schrieber) Geary (centre) at Galt, Ontario (now Cambridge), lowering the colours at the end of the day. Galt was the principal basic training centre for the Women's Royal Canadian Naval Service, and here the Wrens learned the basics of military life. Virtually all Wrens undertook their first months of training here under the stewardship of Commander Isabel McNeil, a much-beloved officer (and sister-in-law to Rear Admiral "Debby" Piers).

Above: A class of WAGs (wireless air gunners) in Edmonton, 1941. WAGs received about seven months of training in wireless operations and six weeks of gunnery training. These men then sat in the Perspex bubbles of heavy bombers to act as the eyes and ears of the aircraft. Their casualty rate was very high, but so were their courage and spirits. Left: The muddy barracks at Debert, Nova Scotia, constructed at the beginning of the war and the staging area for thousands of war-bound soldiers. For most, Debert was the last Canadian base they would see before heading overseas.

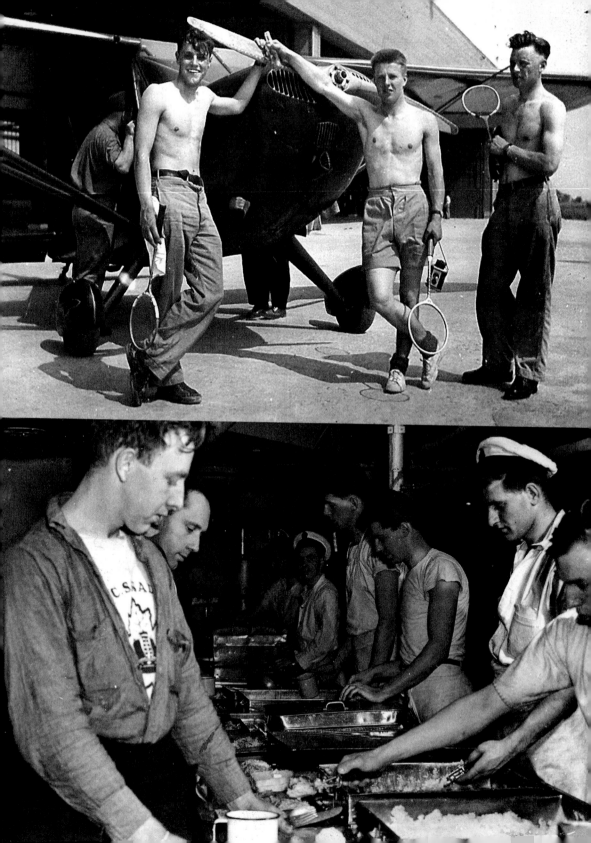

Opposite, top: Badminton in the hangar at Malton, Ontario, in the summer of 1941. Bottom: Lashing out the gash on board HMCS *Prince David*. "Gash" was naval slang for rubbish or garbage from the galley and mess decks. The food on ships wasn't always lousy, but it sure could be.

Above, left: OTU (Operational Training Unit), Silloth, Cumberland, UK. (Clockwise from top) Doug Appleton, Ted Jones, Harry Hawkins, Gordon Miller and Dave Crick. These would be the last few weeks of relative calm before going into "ops." Right, top and bottom: Officers Training Centre (OTC), Brockville, Ontario, summer 1941. Prospective officers got used to messing in the rough.

Left: Dick Hilborn of the 1st Canadian Parachute Battalion leaps from a plane during a practice jump in England. The distinctive protective headgear worn by Canadian (and British) paratroopers early in the war would change when they went into operations, but the volume and weight of their equipment would only increase. Being a paratrooper was not for the faint of heart. Below: An abandoned parachute in Germany, 1945.

Opposite, top: Supper in the field in Normandy. It's been estimated that it took ten servicemen and women to keep one soldier in the front line equipped and fed. Bottom: Joan Thomas (right) and two other nursing sisters embody the life of a nurse in the field.

Above: **June Whiting McRae (right) and two other Wrens walk through Hyde Park in London, 1944. Imagine the exuberant sense of liberation and emancipation these young Canadian women felt not only to be on active service but to travel overseas. Women's place in society was forever changed by the war.**

Opposite, top: **A trench-assault training exercise at Camp Shilo, Manitoba, 1943, that looks all too much like the real thing.** Bottom: **On Sunday-morning manoeuvres against the Home Guard. In the early years of the war, many Canadian troops were stationed on the south coast of England, armed with wooden "weapons" (as the real things were in short supply) to convince German spotters that Allied troops were in full force and well armed.**

Overleaf: **The 2nd Light Anti-Aircraft unit in England, 1942, before embarking for Sicily and the Italian campaign.**

Right: General Eisenhower talking to Canadian soldiers in southeast England shortly before D-Day, spring 1944. Ike's great gifts, according to the men who knew him, were an ability to talk to anyone as an equal and a complete lack of arrogance and pretension. Bottom: A landing craft moving into the Normandy beachhead, escorted by air cover, June 1944. Aircraft flying cover often flew less than fifty feet off the deck.

Opposite: An aerial view of equipment ready to move across the Channel, late May 1944. Photographer Alex Gray could have been court-martialed for taking this photo exposing equipment for the highly secret Operation Overlord, now known as D-Day.

Above: C Squadron Officers' Mess of the Sherbrooke Fusiliers (Armoured Corps), during a Rain Scheme, a training exercise to get the tank corps accustomed to life in the field. Left to right: S.V. "Rad" Radley-Walters (one of the war's finest tank commanders), Clare Thompson, Doug Bradley, Nairn Boyd, and Captain Humphries, spring 1944.

Opposite, top: A village in Normandy after the Germans had evacuated and the Allies were moving through, August 1944. Bottom: In a warehouse outside Amsterdam, holes from the artillery shelling leave a Canadian unit and their vehicles bathed in an unearthly light, March 1945.

Above: Canadian soldiers enter San Pancrazio, Italy, in July 1944. The previous week, German soldiers had massacred all the local men. The instances of such brutality by fanatical German SS-directed units are too numerous to recount; this event barely rates a mention in most histories of the war.

Opposite: A Canadian dispatch rider somewhere in Normandy nonchalantly strikes a match on a mannequin's hip. Alex Gray took this human-interest shot, hoping that this DR's home-town paper might run it. Such pictures gave reassurance to families in Canada that life on the line wasn't without its lighter side.

Left: Corporal Harris of the RCAPC (Royal Canadian Army Pay Corps) finds a spot to rest on a wall of shells in Normandy, an evocative contrast between the picturesque road and the effluence of war. Below, left: Alex Gray wears a German helmet and cleans his nails with a German bayonet, just some of the many souvenirs soldiers found. Below, right: RCA officer Dick Likely had his hair shaved off to combat lice, Italy, 1944.

Opposite: Caen, France, July 1944.

Above, left: **A German medic binds the knee of a young German soldier, both POWs, under the watchful eye of the 1st Canadian Parachute Battalion.** Above, right: **Canadian paratroopers haul some of their supplies in a damaged baby carriage. Any means at hand was employed to move men and equipment.**

Opposite, top: **The first and only beer issued to units prior to night battle at Verrière Ridge, also known as Operation Totalize. This offensive would bring many casualties and much disagreement about its value. The Sherbrooke Fusiliers tank crewmember is airing out his kit and preparing for the upcoming battle.** Bottom: **A shattered Sherman tank of the Sherbrooke Fusiliers. It was hit by alternating armour-piercing (AP) and high-explosive (HE) shells. The turret of the tank was blown straight up and off the body.**

Military signs were essential to achieve some manner of control over the hundreds of thousands of men and machines moving across the Continent. Most signs in battle areas were removed and some would have been altered by the enemy to misdirect Allied troops trying to find their way. Opposite, top right: The sign ironically warns against the taking of photographs in what was surely a battlefield, while the sign on the upper left of this page advertises the services available to Canadian troops at a mobile recreation centre. Opposite, lower right: The German crossroads is the point at which the 1st Canadian Parachute Battalion met up with the Americans in Germany in the final days of the war.

Above: Cruise sign humour against the back-drop of the Elbe taken during the 1st Canadian Parachute Battalion's assault into Germany.

Opposite, top: A field orderly room in Holland, March 1945. Note the "Out-Going Mail" box. Bottom: "London Up" refers to a command position on the Continent, not the city. The maple leaf indicates a Canadian position, and "Up" meant that position was towards the front. Percy Loosemore, who took so many wonderful photographs, is the officer in the middle.

Defeated German soldiers leaving Holland and walking back home to Germany, May 1945. By the war's end, there was virtually no transport for the repatriation of German soldiers, and they were a bedraggled lot as they went on foot through hostile towns and villages that they had occupied as recently as a few weeks earlier.

Above: Russians exchanging civilities with a Canadian paratrooper at a roadblock. Upon reclaiming former enemy territories, Stalin had decreed that his soldiers could wreak unrestrained havoc on the local population for seven days before martial law was reinstated. Even after order was restored, screams of German civilians in the Russian sector were frequently heard during the night. The Canadians could do nothing about this uneasy situation except to hold their line. Left: Defeated German troops awaiting the Allies' permission to continue their walk home.

As Percy Loosemore passed through a German village in May 1945, he was struck by peoples' expressionless faces and was unsure whether they were looking at him or past him. These three schoolgirls caught his eye, with their blonde hair and pale green dresses. As he raised his camera, they ran away frightened, but their teacher spoke to them, and they hesitantly returned to have their picture taken. Their puzzled faces and tentative smiles stayed with him long after he'd moved on down the line.

HMCS *Discovery* Wrens aboard HMCS *Nanaimo* on the occasion of the third anniversary of the Women's Royal Canadian Naval Service.

COMING OF AGE

"You grew up fast."

That statement sums up pretty much everyone's experience during the war. Girls became women, boys became men, innocents became hardened, atheists found God, and simple things became awfully complicated.

Imagine being so young and taking advantage of the irresistible opportunity to see just how much you could do. Tony Griffin, after thirteen weeks of naval training and a few convoys of experience on board a corvette, found himself in St. John's on a ship without a captain. Two had come and gone in a month, but Tony was assured by Admiral Leonard Murray that a new captain would be found as soon as a likely candidate became available. At which point Tony piped up and said, "Sir, let me take her." And after a moment's thought, the Admiral said, "By Jove, I will!"— thus installing Tony as the first "nonprofessional" captain of a major ship of war in Canada.

Such responsibility was a double-edged sword. Veterans' relationships with their families and communities changed at the speed of war. This was not necessarily a bad thing, but the speed of the transformation often outstripped the lives of those left behind. It took the better part of a generation to restore the balance.

Chinese Canadians weren't considered Canadian citizens until 1947, despite their military service. Women who held positions of power in the service were hard pressed to return to the pre-war assumption that a woman's role was to be a homemaker. First Nations soldiers were seen as equals in the service, only to find a less enthusiastic welcome when they were demobbed.

During the war, time seemed compressed and life more intense. Preconceptions were sloughed off like discarded skins and anything seemed possible, both for the good and the bad. During those uneasy years, lifelong bonds were formed, lifelong friends were killed, and a lifetime became a day-to-day affair. Tom Gilday, First Special Service Force, said, "It was all fun and games until the bullets started to fly. If you managed to survive the first five or six hours in combat, you might make it." There wasn't much time to grow up; you were thrown into a very rude and unforgiving world, and if you didn't learn to adapt fast you probably died. As bodies and machines and buildings and nature itself were torn apart, so was the self-assurance of youth.

But even when their expectations weren't fulfilled, the war swept people along so fast that there wasn't time to give it much thought. Young Canadians were tossed into a world that wrenched them from the cockiness of youth into the accountability of war, and sometimes it took the whole of their lives for them to make peace with what had happened.

They came of age much too fast, but they changed the world as the world changed them. You can see it in their faces.

These are photographs of young women and men in the early days of their service. Taken for parents, for friends, or for themselves, the pictures capture the enthusiasm and pride with which this generation enlisted in the various services.

Above: Probationary Wrens Barbara Cousens and Shirley Biggar in sou'westers, aboard HMCS *Protector*, Sydney, Nova Scotia, October 1944.

Opposite: Jim Campbell and his father in Toronto, 1942.

Clockwise from top left: Irene Kendrew, CWAC; Elizabeth Orford, RCAMC physiotherapist; and Trixie (Schrieber) Geary, WRCNS. CWAC was the Canadian Women's Army Corps, RCAMC was the Royal Canadian Army Medical Corps, and WRCNS was the Women's Royal Canadian Naval Service. Only the Royal Canadian Air Force–Women's Division (RCAF–WD) is not pictured. While none of the women's forces were in battle, they were nonetheless frequently in direct peril. They provided essential medical, communication and logistical support services throughout the war, thereby changing the face of the Canadian military.

Opposite: Chow line in the WRCNS mess in Halifax, 1944.

Above: Victor Wong standing to the left of the "Rice Bowl," which was a community fund-raising initiative in Victoria in 1938 to support China's fight against Japan.

Opposite: Victor Wong stands beside a training camp sign with an ironic message, Chilliwack, British Columbia, January 1945. Victor served with the SOE's Force 136. The secrecy of Force 136's work in Burma further obscured Chinese Canadians' contribution to the war effort.

Opposite: Nursing sister Joan Thomas is helped on with her travelling kit in an English field station.

Above, left: Ione Canning, RCAF–WD, telephone (switchboard) operator Eastern Air Command, Halifax. Above, right: Percy Loosemore sits casually on a box of dynamite. Below: Women parachute-packers drying out 'chutes for Canadian paratroopers. Every parachute had to be unpacked, draped, dried and carefully repacked, regardless of whether it had been deployed or not. It was an essential service that was often overlooked, except by those whose lives depended on it.

Opposite, top left: A sign illustrating the objectives for an effective and silent kill, as taught to the 1st Canadian Parachute Battalion. A similar course was taught at Camp X, near Whitby, Ontario, the training ground for espionage agents. Opposite, top right: CTS (combat training school) in Finden, England, December 1944. Bottom: Hand-to-hand combat training with the 1st Canadian Parachute Battalion at Camp Shilo, in Manitoba, 1943.

Above: A paratrooper on a training jump trailing an extra eighty pounds of equipment.

Above: CTS obstacle course, Finden, England, December 1944. This picture: Route march, OTC, Brockville, Ontario, summer 1941.

Opposite: Nita Walt (right), CWAC in London, 1944.

Left and opposite: Obstacle courses. A ghostly double exposure in the photo opposite captures the multitude of challenges thrown at the soldiers. Bottom, left: A Canadian paratrooper uses a motorcycle as an improvised pump to draw water. This kind of ingenuity frequently set the Canadians apart from other services. Bottom, right: Members of the British Women's Land Army wrestle a barrage balloon into position. These balloons were used to deter low-flying aircraft attacks. Their steel cables could be lethal if they snapped loose and lashed the crew handling them.

Above: Sherbrooke Fusiliers grab some much-needed rest on top of their tank.

Opposite: Exhausted 1st Canadian Parachute Battalion troopers sleep during a brief respite from the drive up through Germany in the spring of 1945. In battle, you can exhaust everything—even fear.

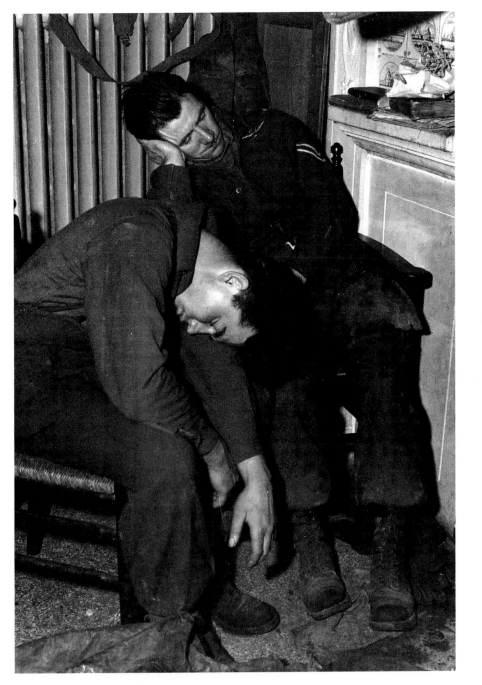

A "bit of a blow" at sea in the North Atlantic onboard HMCS *Prince David*, 1944.

FOR THOSE IN PERIL ON THE SEA

Eternal Father, strong to save,
Whose arm hath bound the restless wave;
Who bidd'st the mighty ocean deep
Its own appointed limits keep;
Oh hear us when we cry to Thee
For those in peril on the sea.

This hymn, written in 1860 after the Reverend William Whiting survived a fierce storm at sea, is played at the close of most naval services of remembrance. Until recently, I was only vaguely aware of its origins and title, but its melody, which ebbs and swells with emotion, was familiar and haunting.

A ship was both a sailor's home and his field of battle. It was a community, a world unto itself, full of its own superstitions, rituals and small, treasured comforts.

The Royal Canadian Navy (RCN), the Royal Canadian Naval Volunteer Reserve (RCNVR), and the Merchant Marine each had its own culture. Life at sea, then, was largely dictated by the service and the ship you found yourself a part of. That, and the weather.

While U-boats and air attacks were deadly threats, most sailors would take a sub attack over foul weather any day of the week, month, or year. Some of the pictures in this section are vivid testaments to the power of storm-tossed seas.

I've found sailors to be quite soulful. While their war was often intense, it was usually against an unseen enemy. They're a special breed: their life at sea demands a willingness to forgo control over their destiny, let alone their comfort. Seamen slung their hammocks over the same tables they ate at and played cards on, but sleep was a luxury, and in high seas the last thing on anyone's mind was a bite to eat.

Surprisingly, many sailors came from the Prairie provinces, and an awful lot of them couldn't swim. George Vant Haaf joined the navy to get away from the bitter Prairie weather, which he said "was ten months winter and two months poor sleighin'." Another sailor said, "Even though I couldn't swim a stroke, I figured leastways the ocean would be flat like the Prairies. It wasn't."

Still, if you had the sea in your blood, there was no other life.

These photographs capture something of what it was like to be at sea during the war: the palpable exhaustion of nonstop watch-keeping; the brutal wrath of an ocean in storm as it battered a ship's superstructure and decks and stripped them bare; the anticipation as you slipped harbour and the peace when you returned.

Romantic and gruelling in equal measures, life aboard ship was a small world in a very large war, and those who were a part of it will always remember splicing the main brace, pier head jumps, and enjoying the comforts of Kye on a midnight watch.

FOR
THOSE
IN PERIL
ON THE
SEA

71

Clockwise from top left: **First Officer Peter Chance on the bridge of HMCS** *St. Thomas*, **a Castle-class corvette; Petty Officer Crabb of HMCS** *Prince David*; **Directional Fire Officer Bill MacDonald in the mid-Atlantic, 1942.**

Opposite: **Jack Burgess (standing) with his crewmates in the mess deck of HMCS** *Niagara*. **These men all saw thousands of hours at sea in their service with the RCN (Royal Canadian Navy) and the RCNVR (Royal Canadian Navy Volunteer Reserve). Life on board ship was not without its discomforts, but these were more than made up for in comraderie and duty towards one's ship and one's shipmates.**

Two perspectives of the threats at sea. Above: The Oerlikon gun crew and lookouts watch the skies on an Atlantic run on board the destroyer HMCS *Chaudière* helmed by Commander Pat Nixon, DSC. Opposite: Hurricane icing on the superstructure of the destroyer HMCS *Saguenay*, January 1942. This kind of ice could easily make a ship top-heavy and threaten her stability in the water. All hands would take turns chopping the ice away in the bitter weather of the North Atlantic.

Scenes of life at sea on board HMCS P*rince David.* Clockwise: Splicing cable in the bosun's stores; A/B (Able Bodied Seaman) Dyck, wearing flash protection, carries a 4-inch artillery shell; Lieutenant Southam, ADO (Air Defence Officer), and Leading Seaman McLaughlin, AA2 (Anti-Aircraft Gunner 2), work on aircraft recognition.

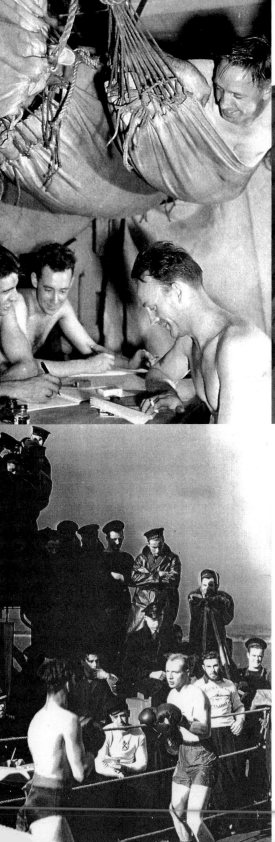

On board HMCS *Iroquois*. Clockwise: Hammocks slung over the table on which the sailors ate, worked and played; sharing a song; a boxing match. When disputes arose at sea a fight would be arranged to let the sailors sort out their disagreement, then they'd shake hands and the matter would be forgotten.

Overleaf: Not dead, only resting. Exhausted seamen on board HMCS *Iroquois*. When there was a short break, sailors would simply find a spot and pass out for a few hours or a few minutes of sleep, but always with their helmets and life vests at hand.

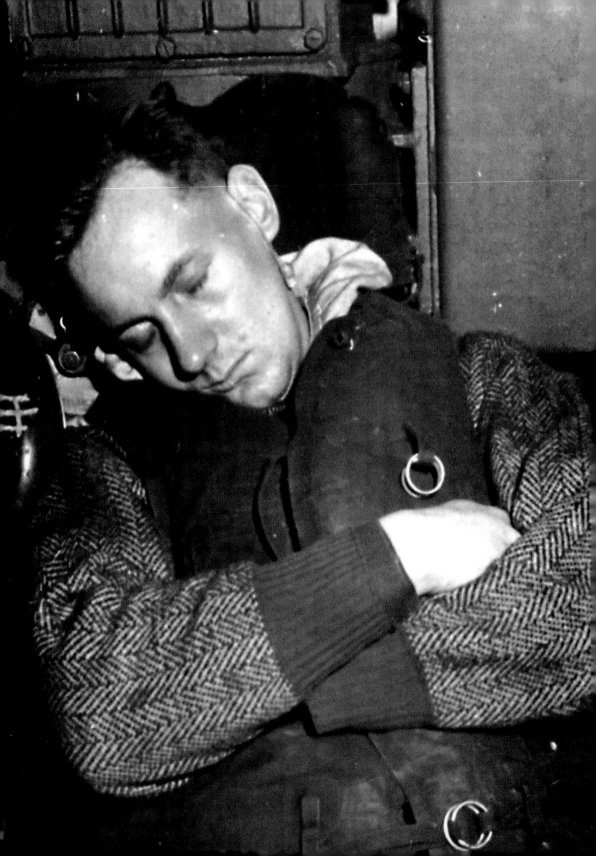

The Flower-class corvette HMCS *Napanee* rolling in fifty-foot swells in the Atlantic. The picture was taken by my cousin, Lt. Jim Melvin, a naval surgeon who was unfortunate enough to have gone to sea on her for this one voyage.

Opposite: **A merchant ship is seen through the sight of a 4-inch gun on board HMCS *Sioux*.**

Above: **HMS *Swift* sinks rapidly off Juno Beach after striking a German mine.** Right: **The sole survivors of the tanker *Conch* are rescued in December 1940. A ship, regardless of her size, could sink with devastating speed when mortally wounded.**

A German U-boat is attacked and sunk from the air by a Sunderland flying boat; the survivors scramble to safety in life rafts off the coast of Ireland. The aircraft was on an anti-sub patrol because an American convoy was coming in, carrying troops for the D-Day invasion. Churchill kept a photograph of the sinking sub in his library, as its sinking was a great success story in the uneasy days before the invasion.

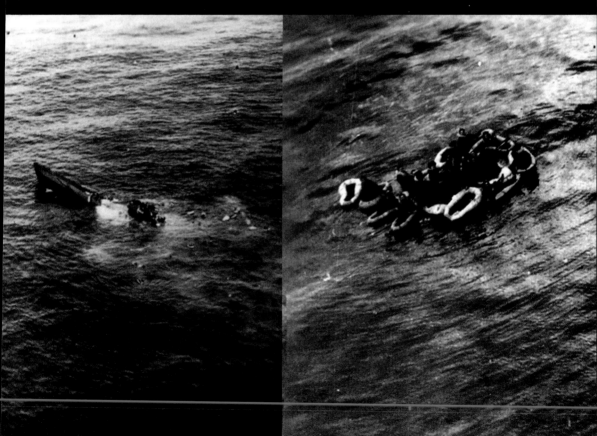

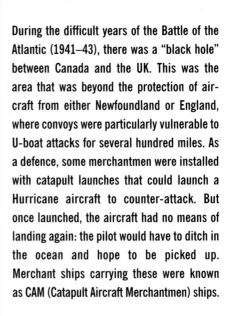

During the difficult years of the Battle of the Atlantic (1941–43), there was a "black hole" between Canada and the UK. This was the area that was beyond the protection of aircraft from either Newfoundland or England, where convoys were particularly vulnerable to U-boat attacks for several hundred miles. As a defence, some merchantmen were installed with catapult launches that could launch a Hurricane aircraft to counter-attack. But once launched, the aircraft had no means of landing again: the pilot would have to ditch in the ocean and hope to be picked up. Merchant ships carrying these were known as CAM (Catapult Aircraft Merchantmen) ships.

A
SOLDIER'S
VIEW

Weather was always an enemy at sea. Opposite: The destroyer HMCS *Chaudière* rolls in heavy weather. On this page, three photos showing the impact of icing on a ship's superstructure. Clockwise from top: HMCS *Pictou*, HMCS *Brandon*, and HMCS *Niagara*.

Overleaf, left: Sunset in the Irish sea. Sometimes the sea could be peaceful and breathtaking. Right, top: Aircraft are ferried to the UK on board HMCS *Puncher*, Canada's only aircraft carrier in World War II. Bottom: A protective barrier is reefed taut to help decelerate aircraft landing on the ship's deck.

Above: August 19, 1942. Personnel landing-craft draw away from a motor torpedo boat to start their run onto the beaches during the raid on Dieppe. A few hours later, a devastated Canadian assault force lay in remnants on the cobbled beach.

Opposite: A Canadian naval ensign flutters over the bodies of Canadian servicemen killed in the landing. Although there are still strong differences of opinion about the reasons behind the failure at Dieppe, the Allies learned a great deal about amphibious landings and about the essential need for the precise coordination of air, ground and naval forces in such an attack. These lessons were later employed with overpowering effect at Normandy.

June 3, 1944; the captain of HMCS *Prince David* gives a final pep talk at Southampton to the ship's crew before loading troops and setting out for Juno Beach.

The senior Protestant naval chaplain gives his blessing to the *Prince David*'s crew later that day. The second Allied front was about to be opened.

Above, left: Early on the morning of June 6, 1944, Le Regiment de la Chaudière leave the *Prince David* and load onto LCTs (Landing Craft, Tank) for their assault on the beach. Above, right: the *Prince David*'s LCAs (Landing Craft, Assault) move towards the beach. Left: LCIs (Landing Craft, Infantry) manoeuvre off the *Prince David*'s stern.

Opposite: On June 6, just a few of the four thousand ships involved in the D-Day invasion can be seen off the Normandy coast. The beachhead had been established, while the *Prince David* held back from the beach in reserve to pick up the inevitable casualties and carry them back to Southampton, England.

The pilot of a Lancaster bomber in 12 Squadron at the controls during a mission. The picture captures a fragment of the world that these pilots inhabited on eight-hour flights over enemy targets. The constant heavy drone of the four Merlin engines and the unheated cockpit made flying a Lancaster an uncomfortable experience; it took strong hands to control the plane, especially when the flying got rough.

DANGEROUS MOONLIGHT

Our first mission was to hit submarine pens in the south of France: there were probably five hundred "heavies" that went in, and the Germans knocked down fifty that night; and for every aircraft that went down, there was about a one-in-ten survival rate.

A ROYAL CANADIAN AIR FORCE BOMB AIMER

Dangerous moonlight is a full moon that makes you an easy target: just one of the risks of flying over enemy territory at night. Flying in wartime was always a risky business, and the RCAF had one of the highest mortality rates of any service.

In training, an inexperienced pilot could turn a crew of seven into a ball of fire by simply misjudging his aircraft's capabilities. Early in the war, fighter pilots had a life expectancy of about six hours in combat. Technology was constantly being outstripped by demand, and machines frequently went into action before their gremlins had been sorted out.

If you were lucky enough to survive flying through icing up in bad weather on a midnight bombing run, you still had to work with limited navigational equipment to find your way to your target where German anti-aircraft flak lay in wait.

By all accounts, the flak took some getting used to. "What the hell was I thinking when I said I wanted to fly?" recalled one navigator after first seeing the tracers and explosions reaching four miles up into the night sky as his crew flew into a cloud of fire and shrapnel at 250 mph.

If luck were against you, the searchlights would "cone" you in a triangulation of blinding light. One bomber pilot described it: "There'd be ten or twelve searchlights that would join up and lock you in the apex of all the beams. The interior of your plane would be so bright that you literally couldn't see anything. You were totally dazzled. Once they coned you, the flak opened up and usually that was that.

"We only got coned once, but it was with a full bomb load. When it happened, I stuck the nose of the aircraft straight down. We must have dove five or six thousand feet straight down, then twisted, turned and pulled, hoping we weren't hit by someone else's bombs or plane. We were lucky."

Bombers also had to dodge night fighters. They'd creep up behind and below the aircraft to rake it with their upward firing cannons. Les Wallace recalls one such terrible trip in March 1945. "A fighter flare was dropped above and ahead of us, which made us sitting ducks, but we managed to evade being hit and carried on to Nuremberg, our target. Just before we got there, a night fighter caught us and took out our rear turret and our outer port engine; but we didn't know that yet, so we kept going. By the time we reached the target area, we had suffered considerable damage from the flak and were losing height. Then our inner starboard engine caught fire and with the damage we'd sustained, I knew we were going down.

"Our Wireless Op went to check on damage and found that our rear turret gunner, Ray, had been seriously injured, which ruled out the possibility of everyone bailing out; so we decided to stick it out together. My engineer warned me that we were in danger of losing a third engine that was overheating and we were down to four thousand feet. We managed to make contact with a small American fighter landing strip near Reims in France. They guided us to this small patch of grass intended for fighters only; we touched down nearly two-thirds of the way near the end, winding up straddling railroad tracks with a train coming our way. But the Americans stopped it in time and Ray pulled through. That was a close one."

It was also the exception. The casualty rate was as high as seven out of ten on bomber command. But that didn't really seem to faze anyone.

Spitfire pilot Art Sager ran out of bullets in a dogfight with a Messerschmitt, then shook his fist in fury at the German pilot, daring him to take his best shot. Another Spit pilot, Ian Ormston, cartwheeled down the runway in a wounded "kite." Ormy broke his back, but his only regret was having to return to Canada as a flight instructor after six months in a body cast. Like all of the airmen I spoke to, he wanted nothing more than to get back up there again.

"It was better than… well, it's better than sex," one flyer said to me. Most of them would still be flying now, sixty years later, if they could. Some of them still are.

Left: Pilot Officer Jim Kenny in the cockpit of his rocket-firing Typhoon. This plane was originally designed as a high-altitude fighter-bomber, but in practice it excelled as a ground-attack aircraft. Below, left: Flight Sergeant Loudfoot on the wing of a Gypsy Moth, the plane on which most pilots received their elementary training (as well as on her successor, the Tiger Moth). Below, right: The pilot and navigator from Marcel Croteau's Lancaster of 425 "Alouette" Squadron, a French-Canadian squadron in 6 Bomber Group. Marcel was a cowboy from Alberta, but he was crewed up with the Alouettes. Although he had little in common with the "Easterners" apart from the French language, his crew became a tight fighting unit.

A Gypsy Moth trainer in England in 1941.
These biplanes were described as being "as
safe as a church" by one pilot. They could land
at low airspeeds, and manoeuvred well in the
air. Ex-RCAF fighterpilot Dick Corbett says that
if he had one today, he'd still be flying.

Opposite: **Vern Williams inside a Fairey Battle fighter-bomber at Jarvis Bombing and Gunnery School, 1940. A promising aircraft in the 1930s, the Fairey Battle was removed from operations in September 1940 and used for training in Britain and Canada throughout the war.**

Above: **This was the pilot's first flight over enemy territory, and he excitedly told everyone in the squadron about his encounter with an enemy aircraft, a rite of passage for a novice fighter pilot.** Left: **Wireless air gunner Wally Loucks (left) and his crew study a map for their upcoming mission. His was the first all-Canadian bomber crew to complete a tour of "ops" in 1944.**

Opposite: Alex Gray carries a large-format camera for taking detailed pictures from the air. His work as an RCAF photographer took him to all areas of the force's operations, and many of the finest photographs in this book are from his collection.

Left: A Typhoon squadron horsing around in Normandy, 1944. Alex Gray described them as "a hell of a nice bunch—tough buggers." Many of the men shown here were killed in action a short time after this photo was taken.
Below: The ground crew of Art Sager's Spitfire flight, 421 Squadron, in Kenley, Surrey. The ground crew was an essential part of any squadron; they maintained the planes as if they were their own.

Opposite: A crew from 14 Squadron, in North Africa. They were a mixture of Canadians, Australians, South Africans, New Zealanders, and even a few Brits.

Above: Dick Corbett (left) and his squadron mates from 11 Squadron in India, 1943. Their theatre of operations was Burma, where Dick was eventually shot down and became a POW under his Japanese captors.

Above: "Bombing up" a Lancaster. The routine was practised by all bomber crews: each bomb was winched into its place in the bay; its fuses were checked, and its supports tested.

Opposite: A crew waiting to be bombed up before a raid. Wing Commander Buck Buchanan (centre) was Commanding Officer of 14 Squadron. Buchanan was a legendary character and commonly referred to as "Mad Buck" Buchanan. By the time of his death, he had completed approximately eight hundred bomber operations. He worked this crew so hard that he started to use two crews. He led every bomber operation the squadron was detailed for. He was eventually shot down over the Aegean Sea with the crew shown here. According to his crewmates who survived, Buchanan seemed to have burned out and lost his desire to live. He died in the life raft and they slipped his body into the water.

Left: Bomber crews were often taken from their base to their aircraft on lorries driven by members of the RAF-WD. In a pinch, the women were known to give the crews a lungful of pure oxygen to clear their heads for their mission, if they were feeling unwell either from illness or from a drop too much celebration the night before. Below, left: A flight of Lancasters marshalled for night takeoff in England, 1945. You can see the line of bombers stretching back for miles. Below, right: On the airstrip of Castle Camps, Cambridgeshire, where 410 Squadron, an RCAF Mosquito unit, was stationed from 1942 to the end of the war.

Jack Gouinlock's Halifax "N for Natch." This photo was taken shortly before he was shot down over Belgium. Virtually all planes were named and decorated with "nose art," and with a graphic count of the numbers of missions flown (indicated here by the bombs painted beneath the cockpit).

A flight of Venturas over Pennfield Ridge, New Brunswick. Pennfield Ridge was part of the British Commonwealth Air Training Plan, and was an OTU (operational training unit) that gave aircrews their final training before they went overseas and into operations. The pilots and crews were being trained for low-level daylight bombing operations. The Ventura was a reconnaissance bomber that was used largely for maritime and training operations.

Opposite: An Allied plane bombs tanks and armoured vehicles in the North African desert, in a photo taken from a height of four thousand feet. Aerial bombing operations in North Africa were less well known than land operations, but they were essential in keeping the Germans from taking control of the Mediterranean region.

Above: A lone British bomber flies over the city of Dieppe after the battle has already been lost on August 19, 1942. The raid's original July date was aborted, and the Germans had increased their defences sixfold by August. The Allies sustained substantial naval, army and air force losses.

Opposite, top: Hugh Godefroy's Spitfire, part of the renowned 401 Squadron, seen here flying over Kent in 1942. The 401 was a RAF fighter squadron crewed almost entirely by Canadians. Bottom, left: Ian "Ormy" Ormston, one of a close-knit group of pilots in 401 who kept in close contact with one another through the sixty years after the war's end. John "Scruffy" Weir was also a part of this exceptional group. Bottom, right: Vapour trails of a dogfight over France, 1944. Dogfights usually lasted only a few minutes, but in a windless sky the aircraft's paths could hang in the air indefinitely.

Above: An Allied fighter pilot lands after bailing out from his burning Spitfire following a dogfight, 1944.

Above: A view out the cockpit window of a flight of Lancasters on a bombing run over Germany, 1944.

Opposite, top: A shot from inside the cockpit of an Anson during a training flight in Canada. Originally designed in 1935, the Anson was too small for utility or coastal patrol, but was adapted for use as a multi-role trainer. Most Canadian pilots flew this solid, stable aircraft sometime during their training. Bottom: A view from the mid-upper turret looking back towards the tail of a Lancaster during a bombing mission over Germany, 1944. Although these positions were vulnerable to attack from enemy aircraft, you could not ask for a finer view.

Opposite: A clear shot of a bombing run training exercise. The triangular shape of the target can be seen in the wake of the aircraft.

Above: A bombing mission over France. Unlike the low-level target-practice bombing mission pictured opposite, this photo shows the kinds of heights from which heavy bombers dropped their load of bombs. This photograph is from 617 Squadron, aka "The Dam Busters," who practised until they could hit a target from as high as twenty thousand feet with an error margin of about twenty yards.

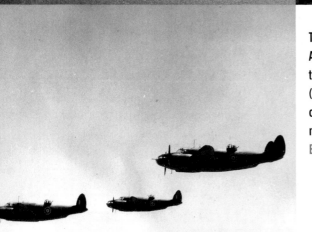

The beauty of airplanes. Top, left and opposite: A flight of Harvards, which were primarily training aircraft. Top, right: A Mossie (Mosquito Bomber), one of the great airplanes of the war. It was a hot rod to fly and a huge number were manufactured in Canada. Bottom, left: A flight of Venturas.

Vern Williams (left) and his pilot, Joe Schultz,
describing how he manoeuvred them out of a
particularly tight encounter with a night fighter. Vern and Joe were the two-man crew of a
Mosquito fighter. Returning to England after
an intruder operation over Europe, they
crossed paths with a flight of German
bombers returning from an attack. When
they'd run out of ammunition, Vern and Joe
debated returning to base or trying to ram
one of the German aircraft mid-air. They
decided it made more sense to live to fight
another day.

CNT RXAF23   32 2 EXTRA GB RCAF OTTAWA ONT 8
0369
MISTER H W CHENEY REPORT DELIVERY
24 WENDOVER AVE OTTAWA

M9248 REGRET TO ADVISE THAT YOUR SON FLYING OFFICER DONALD
HARRY CHENEY J ONE EIGHT TWO NINE FIVE IS REPORTED MISSING
AFTER AIR OPERATIONS OVERSEAS AUGUST FIFTH STOP LETTER
FOLLOWS

RCAF CASUALTIES OFFICER

THE FACE OF BATTLE

The experiences of each branch of the service were distinctly their own, of course. Sailors said they couldn't imagine being stuck in a trench or having someone shoot at them huddled inside an aircraft twenty thousand feet in the air. Aircrews didn't want to be earthbound, let alone adrift at sea, and fighter pilots didn't want to have to be responsible for anyone's flying but their own. And ground troops, also known as the PBI (poor bloody infantry), embodied a curious mixture of knowing that their job was to walk into the face of the enemy and a desire not to have it any other way. There were also those who had little control over how their war unfolded: nursing sisters, supply services personnel, POWs, special-operations agents and, perhaps most tragically, the civilians who found themselves caught in the crossfire. War spares no one.

As one battle-hardened veteran observed, "In battle, some are lucky, some aren't. You heard a machine-gun bullet go this way, then another one that way. Someone next to you was killed, someone was wounded over to your right. When that happened, you couldn't stop and help. At best, you gave him a shot of morphine or something if you could. Because in battle you've got to keep moving.

"So you patted your wounded pal on the shoulder and said, 'I'll see you soon, you lucky bastard. You're going to be back in England with all those lovely nurses,' when you knew damned well he was going to die."

On another day and at another battle, Gerry Goddard was moving from his landing craft up onto Juno Beach hauling his Bren gun on his shoulder when he saw men from his unit just lying there on the sand. "What are they doing?" he thought. "Resting?" It didn't make any sense. As the day unfolded and the casualty numbers were taken, Gerry was the only Bren gunner and one of only twenty-five of his company of 130 men who survived that first battle of D-Day.

In the summer of 1941, the Germans invaded and captured Crete, thereby controlling the eastern Mediterranean. Some Allied soldiers were asked to volunteer to stay behind and harass the Germans using guerrilla warfare tactics. One such soldier who later managed to escape took these extraordinary pictures of the German paratroop invasion.

Above: A view from the bridge of the destroyer HMCS *Sioux* as it fired 40-mm anti-aircraft twin mounts against an air attack. Left: A German submarine surfaces off the starboard bow of a destroyer while being hunted in the North Atlantic, 1943.

Opposite: On July 2, 1940, the SS *Arandora Star* was carrying German and Italian detainees to Canada, along with her British crew. She was torpedoed by a German U-boat north of Ireland shortly after dawn. This picture shows a few of the 861 survivors rescued by HMCS *St. Laurent* seven hours after the ship sank.

Below: Lancaster pilot Geoff Marlow looks back over his shoulder towards the navigator's position.

Opposite: A Halifax bomber on a run and facing the worst kind of trouble. Her engines are on fire and she has only a short time before she goes down. With luck, the pilot would be able to keep her stable and aloft long enough for the crew to bail out. The pilot's job was to stay at the controls until everyone was out. We do not know whether this pilot or his crew successfully escaped a fiery death.

Opposite: Taken the morning after an air raid in 1940; a woman and child stare at the empty place where their house had stood the night before in London's East End.

Above: Nita Walt (right), CWAC, in London, February 28, 1943, observing fire and bomb damage from German raids. This was often the first taste of war that Canadians had when arriving from overseas. Right: In the East End of London, 1941.

A German soldier walks across the strand at Dieppe, August 19, 1942. A German photographer took this and many other photographs on that day. This shot captures something of the complete destruction that the Canadian forces suffered.

Above, left: Padre Laurie Wilmot and his batman in Italy, shortly before going into a catastrophic battle in late August 1943 at the Gothic Line. Above, right: A common sight in the Italian campaign: a house riddled with shell holes, on the road to Ortona. Left: Canadian soldiers hold their position on Via Michele Bianchi (known today as Via della Libertà), near the sporting grounds of Ortona.

Opposite: Soldiers searching for a German sniper, Montespertoli, Italy, July 27, 1944. The photograph gives some idea of the massive destruction that occurred in the Italian mountain towns. The Germans had dug in and had to be cleared out one house at a time.

Overleaf, left: A series of five photographs taken by a German photographer. The German machine-gun position wounds Canadian soldiers during their attempt to cross the Moro River. Right: Sniper Private Jack Bailey of the Perth Regiment looks over Orsogna, Italy, January 29, 1944. Being a sniper was a specialized and dangerous role in the front lines; his keen eye could wreak havoc on enemy troops, but he had to take great care not to draw too much fire in response. One sniper I spoke to said it was "like hunting deer back home, and I started to enjoy the sport of it a little too much."

Above: Soldiers of Le Régiment de la Chaudière leave HMCS *Prince David* and load onto a landing craft for their assault on Juno Beach, June 6, 1944. Opposite: A lookout on duty onboard HMCS *Prince David* scans the beach as the landing craft go in to Juno on D-Day. Spread: A small fraction of the Allied armada crosses the English Channel for the invasion of Normandy. Troop ships and landing craft are visible, and barrage balloons fly overhead to deter attack from enemy fighters.

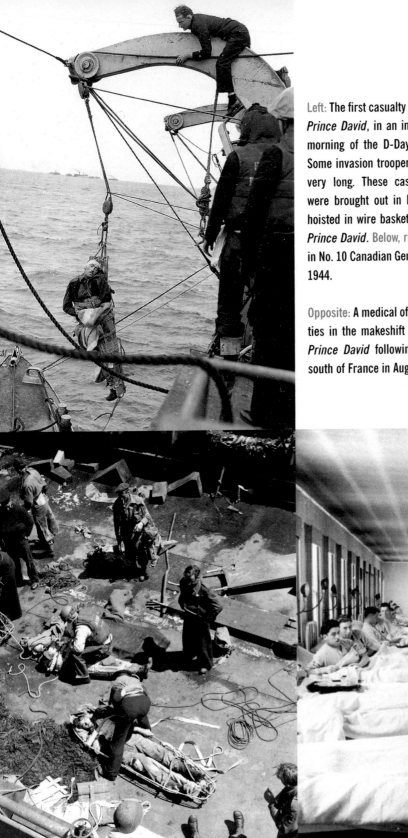

Left: The first casualty is taken onboard HMCS *Prince David*, in an improvised sling, on the morning of the D-Day invasion. Below, left: Some invasion troopers didn't stay in France very long. These casualties and survivors were brought out in landing craft and then hoisted in wire baskets to the deck of HMCS *Prince David*. Below, right: The casualty ward in No. 10 Canadian General Hospital, England, 1944.

Opposite: A medical officer attends to casualties in the makeshift medical bay on HMCS *Prince David* following the landings in the south of France in August 1944.

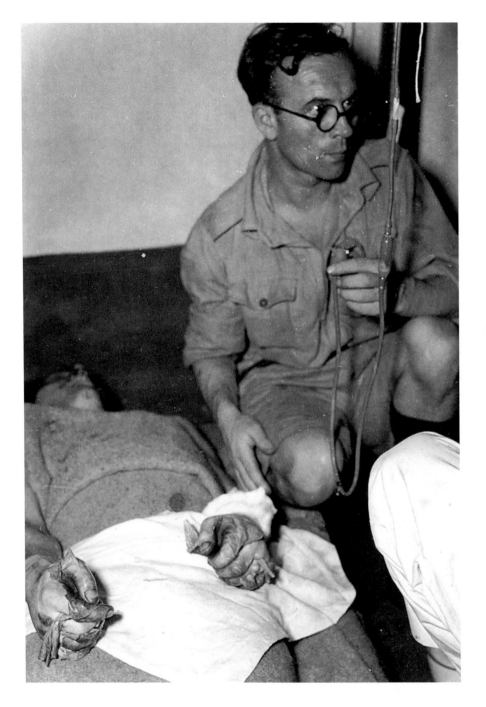

Paratroopers fight through the villages and towns in and around Arnhem, Holland, during operation Market Garden, September 1944. The Germans were well dug in, the fighting was intense, and Allied casualties were high. It was street-fighting at its worst: running from doorway to doorway, scrambling for cover in trenches and artillery craters, all the while trying to maintain communications with malfunctioning radios.

Above: The 1st Canadian Parachute Battalion moves into action for the Crossing of the Rhine, March 1945. With lessons learned from Market Garden and D-Day, the Rhine assault was a carefully planned attack, with such good intelligence and preparation that, in the daylight landing, the paratroopers were able to land accurately in their designated DZs (drop zones) and to easily recognize their objectives. The war's end was now in sight.

Opposite: Even the Rhine assault had its casualties. A 1st Canadian Parachute Battalion trooper lies dead in a field. German machine gunners shot the invading Canadian soldiers as they descended on the DZ.

Above: The carnage of battle is visible in this photograph, taken during the Battle of Normandy. Bodies, vehicles, animal carcasses and the overpowering smell of death were memories that no soldier from the Normandy campaign will ever forget.

Opposite: A sniper with the 1st Canadian Parachute Battalion stands over the body of his first German "kill." The expression on his face is one of resignation: he took no pride in killing an enemy soldier; it was a necessary act of war. This small-town Canadian boy was caught up in many more such abhorrent scenes, and after his return to Canada after the war, he severed all associations with his former unit and rarely ever spoke of the war again.

Left to right: German paratroopers killed by the Van Doos; two images of Germans killed after the Canadian battle at Moerbrugge, three miles from Brugge, Belgium; and a shattered German soldier in Arnhem.

Right: A German Panzer taken out of action near Caen, France, July 1944. Below, left: The 1st Canadian Parachute Battalion as they move into Germany. The troopers are immediately behind the front line. Below, right: A Canadian Sherman tank resting near Canadian graves near Caen during the Battle of Normandy.

Opposite: A signpost near the German border for Operation Veritable, the battle of the Reichswald Forest, one of the last brutal stands of the Germany army, February 1945. It was a scene of rain, mud, and constant shelling. Spacing between vehicles was essential to minimize damage from artillery fire.

Above: A member of the Dutch Underground covers the dead bodies of Dutch hostages executed the previous night alongside an Amsterdam canal, 1944. Germans soldiers can be seen patrolling across the water. German reprisals against the Underground continued until the very last hours of the occupation of the Netherlands. Left: French resistance fighters (the Maquis). It was not unheard of for collaborators to pose as Maquis and to inform the enemy of Allied troop positions.

This photograph shows the destruction of a Belgian collaborator's home in Brugge after its liberation by the Canadians in September 1944. Reprisals ranged from trashing personal belongings and shaving heads to a pistol shot in the back of the head.

Above: Three German prisoners of war being searched by Canadian soldiers and members of the Belgian Brigade in Sallenelles, France, August 17, 1944.

Opposite: At the war's end, three Hitler Jugend, or Hitler Youth, released from the front and walking back to Germany, met up with Percy Loosemore. He raised his camera to take the photo, and one of them shouted, "Nein! Nein!" But the other two restrained him, and Percy shot this picture.

Bob Mullin (second from right), RCA Signals and Airborne, with friends and extended family in England, 1941. One of the great pleasures for Canadian servicemen in the UK was the chance to meet relatives, or to be "adopted" by local families. Pubs across the UK adopted whole crews and platoons as their own, and the pub became a warm and welcoming source of comfort, information, and consolation.

IN FAITHFUL COMPANY

We few, we happy few, we band of brothers;
For he today that sheds his blood with me
Shall be my brother.

Friendship, companionship, love, and loss were inextricably intertwined during the war. Connections were made that would last a lifetime, and those who served together often speak of these relationships as the closest of their lives.

One RCAF pilot spoke about his crew who had disbanded sixty years earlier. They flew a handful of tours of duty together; they bunked, ate, griped, and socialized together. But when the time came near the end of the war to go their separate ways, they packed up their kits and never saw one another again. When I asked him why, the best answer he could offer, even as he wept at the memory, was that they were afraid of outliving such special friendships.

In the service, and particularly in combat, men and women discovered a new vocabulary of thought and feeling. "Fighting for the chance to get shot at," was one ironic observation. "I couldn't believe the bastards shot me," was another. George Blackburn remembers "terrible fatigue; that's the saving grace. You can be so damned tired that the prospect of eternal sleep isn't that bad."

In such intense times, the company of friends and loved ones was a powerful and unifying force. Sometimes even a pet dog or cat could provide important companionship, their simple needs offering comfort and their affection a welcome distraction.

Friends raised hell together, sometimes just to ease the tension. One pilot flew his Tiger Moth up Yonge Street in Toronto; a bunch of Cape Breton Highlanders grabbed their Bren gun one night and raked the top of an RCAF Nissen hut in Nova Scotia. While each service tended to look down on the others, their antics bound them together as a squadron, a crew, or a unit. (And the Cape Bretoners were a tough bunch.)

You had your picture taken with your buddies, you got your tattoos at the same time, and you wore your unit's flashes with pride: you were connected to something bigger than yourself and smaller than the world at war.

Sharing a pint and a laugh with someone who'd survived what you'd been through forged an unbreakable bond that lasted longer than pretty much anything else in life.

I'd never want to go through all the heartbreak and horror that so many vets came to know, but I can see the joy of life and of friendship that they treasure as a result.

This, above all, I envy them.

Overleaf, left: **Merv Couse (right), an RCAF navigator, with his best friend, Freddy, who was killed shortly afterwards in a circuit-and-bump training exercise in England.** Right: **Bob Dixon (right) of the RCA with his best friend in his unit in Italy. They slipped into a photographer's studio on leave during the Italian campaign and had their portrait taken together, probably for the price of a pack of cigarettes.**

Opposite: **A couple of young Fusiliers Mont-Royal troopers clowning around in the early days of training.**

Right: **Three able-bodied seamen striking a casual pose for the camera when their ship was in port.** Below, left: **Two SPs (Sea Patrol) gently lead a sailor who blew off a little bit too much steam on shore leave, back to base.** Below, right: **On board HMCS *Iroquois*, sailors pay tribute to the leadership of the German armed forces.**

Faithful friends and family. Opposite, top:
Corporal Langley and "Snowy" Bridges share
a quiet drink in Holland at the war's end.
Bottom: Brothers in arms: Wally Loucks,
RCAF wireless air gunner (left) and Merv
Loucks, 1st Canadian Parachute Battalion. Of
First Nations heritage, both men served with
distinction through the war. Above: Florence
Pennington (right) and her two sisters, 1944.
The women were in different branches of the
military, but they all shared the pride of their
father's service in World War I.

Above, left: Some of the first draft of CWACs in British Columbia, January 1942. Early enlistees didn't have uniforms or proper barracks to live in. Above, right: Lee Grainger, RAF–WD in Yorkshire, May 1943. Grainger was one of the many RAF-WDs who served alongside the numerous Canadian squadrons stationed in the north of England. Left: A WAAF (Women's Auxiliary Air Force) in Wattisham, Suffolk, who went by the name of "Dimples" for self-evident reasons.

A photograph of an English servicewoman found on the beach at Dieppe amongst the few belongings of a Canadian soldier who had been killed. Nothing is known of her or of the boy who carried her picture.

Opposite, top: In North Africa, *Life* magazine war correspondent Morley Lester-Brooks talks to two members of 14 Squadron. Morley was attached to the squadron for several weeks and a passenger on several raids. Bottom: Members of an RCAF touring entertainment unit wait to take their turn in the outdoor facilities in Labrador, 1944.

Below: Nora Cook, a Royal Canadian Army Medical Corps nurse, enjoys a picnic lunch, improvised from rations, with a friend in England, shortly before embarking for service in a field hospital in France.

My uncle, Bill MacAskill, drink in hand, shares some good times with friends and some young Dutch women in a Canadian mess, at the war's end.

A photograph of Eileen, the war bride of Sherbrooke Fusilier Ed Haddon. Ed carried her photograph, and one of his mother, throughout the war. Such small connections with home could raise the spirits when the span of distance and time seemed interminable.

Faithful friends. Opposite, clockwise: HMCS *Swansea*'s mascots; a Wren's feline mascot "Bunts," short for "bunting tosser," a nickname given to WRCNS signallers; the remarkable Newfoundland dog Gander, embarking for Hong Kong with the Royal Rifles of Canada. Gander would serve with distinction, earning the Dickin Medal, the equivalent of a Victoria Cross for animals; Hughie Godefroy of 401 Squadron and his puppy enjoying a warm summer's day in Kent, England.

Above: This starving pup was found alongside the road by Dick Likely's RCA unit as they moved north through Italy. He was much loved by the men, who adopted him and brought him back to strength. When he died, he was given a military burial with full honours.

Above: Chinese Canadians of Force 136 SEAC (Southeast Asia Command) at Singarh Mountain, the British army camp near Poona, India, 1945.

Opposite, top: Lieutenant Jim Hay, DSC (left), and Petty Officer Gray, DSM (right), with the ASDIC team of the destroyer HMCS *Chaudière*, under Commander Pat Nixon. Bottom: Officers in the basement bomb shelter of London House, a residence in London for officers of all services stationed there during the war. Front row, second from the right, is my grandfather Eric Heathcote, and his good friend Don Sutherland (back row, left). Don, a gentle, unassuming man, undertook extraordinarily dangerous work in mine disposal for the Navy, and went on to train a Canadian commando unit that was to land at Juno Beach under cover of darkness to destroy German defences in preparation for the landings. These officers all served in senior intelligence or command positions in London, kindred spirits fortuitously living in the same welcoming home.

Opposite, top: RCAF men billeted at Stornoway on the Isle of Lewis enjoying a private party. A keg of whisky had gone missing, and the man charged with tracking it down can be seen sitting to the left of the keg in question. Five hours later, he "discovered" the empty keg at the side of a road and duly reported it to his superiors. Bottom: The Master's Den pub in Eccles, outside of Manchester, Yorkshire. Bill MacDonald (second from right), RCNVR, looks happily towards the sky, content with his pint and good company to while away an afternoon off duty.

Above: My grandfather has a pint on the outside porch of the Prospect of Whitby in the East End of London. The pub received its name in Dickens's time, in honour of a popular nearby landmark, the Whitby collier (a type of ship) called The Prospect, which was moored outside for many years. A hangman's yardarm and noose overhang the Thames just to the right of the pints of Guinness on the gallery's railing.

Opposite: Bert Coles (kneeling, at left) exercises his considerable abilities at "African golf," or craps to the uninitiated. Bert was an RCAF pilot with 14 Squadron, which flew hundreds of missions over North Africa and the Mediterranean.

Above: 401 Squadron pilots "running in loose formation" in Kent, 1943. Left: Peter Chance and his new bride, Peggy Barker, a Wren wireless telegraphist, celebrate their wedding on board the destroyer HMCS *Skeena* moored in Plymouth, England, September 1944. They had a brief five-day respite from the war as a honeymoon before both returned to their duties.

Above: Alex Jardine (centre) and his crew on a "pleasure cruise" at Nancowry Island, India, in 1940. Left: Bert Coles and his squadron arrived at Gambut, Libya, on December 24, 1941, where they took over a captured German aerodrome, which provided them with better conditions than they had previously experienced living in the desert. They had a mess tent for meals, an operations shack, and decent tents—all of which, of course, were German-made. When they ran out of decent clothes, they wore German breeches, stockings, and other items.

Tony Craven (far left) and his crew in the Middle East, 1943. The desert war was a tough life. It was hot and dusty in the daytime, cold and pitch black at night; water was extremely scarce; scorpions and other insects drove the men mad; and distractions or diversions were to be found only in distant towns and villages.

From top to bottom: Peter Briscoe, RCAF navigator/bomb aimer (second from right) and his crew under the wing of their plane with 194 Squadron in Burma, 1943; Morden Walker snapped this photo of fellow engineers in Normandy, 1944. These little-heralded men were often right at the front lines, digging in, clearing out, and taking heavy fire from the enemy as they cleared, built, and foraged their way into battles in bulldozers and machinery meant for construction, not war; A regimental dinner of Les Fusiliers Mont-Royal (taken by Pierre Faribault) in Berlin, July 1945; A football game using unconventional gear in the North African desert with pilots from 238 Squadron on Christmas Day, 1943.

From top to bottom: Dick Field's RCA unit during the Battle of the Scheldt, 1944; 1st Canadian Parachute Battalion troopers having a break in Germany, 1945; Marcel Croteau's 425 "Alouette" Squadron receiving a gift from the French in thanks for the squadron's assistance in the liberation of their country, July 14, 1944; American GIs crossing the Channel on HMCS *Prince David*, watching for their first sight of the coast of France, July 4, 1944.

Nora Cook (right) and other nurses in the mud outside of Ward 12 at a field hospital in France, 1944.

Bill Jenkins (far left) with other members of
the 1st Canadian Parachute Battalion during
their move into Germany, 1945.

Above: **A Canadian naval officer offers a light to a member of the French Maquis, 1944.**

Opposite: **Harold Ridley and Ken Ball of 14 Squadron looking dashingly sun-bleached and tousled while restlessly waiting for their next operation in the North African desert, 1943.**

St.-Niklaas Kerk photographed from within the workings of a facing clock tower, in the medieval city of Ghent, Belgium, 1945. Belgium was spared the widespread destruction that Holland experienced and the soldiers stationed there at the war's end enjoyed seeing the sights.

ACCIDENTAL TOURISTS

Except for a privileged few, a trip abroad was something of a rarity seventy years ago. So imagine the exhilaration of growing up in rural Saskatchewan or small town Quebec and getting the chance to travel and see the world at government expense—maybe not always in the most comfortable of circumstances, but at a time when the world was in motion.

Kit Graham of the 8th Canadian Hussars found himself near Naples at the foot of Mount Vesuvius.

"By golly, after we got through the business of getting there, there was Vesuvius! We'd read about it in school. Gee, that was great. So we climbed . . . well, crawled . . . up as far as we could and looked down the volcano's mouth, a quarter of a mile across. Pretty neat. Then a month or so later we were back in that area and Vesuvius was in full eruption. Exploding God knows how many thousands of feet in the air and the ash fallout was violet, gentian violet. On one of our regular route marches in the days that followed, we came back and the ash kept piling up on our helmets, arms and shoulders, all violet. You couldn't wash that stuff out, so we had to junk our clothes. But we got to see Vesuvius in action."

Often veterans didn't know what it was they were seeing. Red Martin found himself having a look around Rome shortly after its liberation in 1944. He avoided the cluster of soldiers around one spot, sceptical of what could be so important. It was the Sistine Chapel. Before he left

Italy, Red, a Presbyterian boy, was granted an audience with Pope Pius XII. When the Pope offered his hand, Red, being first in line, shook it, smiled, and wished him well.

Dick Likely went up the Eiffel Tower at the war's end and took a snapshot of a US bomber plane sitting in the plaza below rather than the normal tourist shot of the Parisian skyline. A soldier's sensibilities couldn't help but shape his perspective on the world, even long after the war was past.

Bill MacAskill, my uncle, took a snapshot of Berlin's Brandenburg Gate just a few weeks after the end of the war. The picture's rough qualities capture the turbulent and uneasy mood of that shattered city.

Moody Parisian skylines, the sun-bleached dust of the desert, the abrupt and frozen landscapes on the Murmansk Run, even postcard-pretty street scenes: these are pictures taken in celebration of what war had failed to destroy.

Above: RCA trooper Ken Lataboudieau on sentry duty near the coastal batteries on the west coast of Canada, surely one of the most beautiful spots in the country to stand guard.

Opposite: Bombardier Bud Garrett, RCA Signals, on the island launch *York*. This boat was used to bring supplies to the Yorke Island Battery from Kelsey Bay, Vancouver Island.

Allerton Castle, Yorkshire. Steeped in history, the castle served as HQ for 6 Bomber Group RCAF. It is also the ancestral home of Lord Mowbray and is the most important Gothic Revival castle in England.

Right: A pastoral scene at a stately country home, England, 1943. One of the great pleasures of Canadian service members stationed in England was being able to travel to virtually any part of the UK at little or no expense. One can well imagine what a calming break a scene like this would be from combat duty or from the constant air raids in the cities. Below: A beautiful cobbled street running alongside a pub in Yorkshire, where so many bomber squadrons were based. One navigator described how their local pub adopted the whole crew, conveyed news to their families in Canada, and even provided accommodation and consolation after the war for visiting bereaved parents.

Opposite: The *Prince David* arrived at its anchorage in the Solent off the Isle of Wight, near Portsmouth. This photograph, taken on April 15, 1944, is of the coastline near Freshwater. The Isle of Wight was a very active place during the war, and many amphibious landing training schemes were undertaken there.

Below: War changed many things, but not Eton. This photo was taken near Windsor Castle, which overlooks the playing fields of the exclusive boys' school whose uniforms have changed little over the years, or even over the centuries.

For Canadians stationed in the UK, there was much to see, and wandering the streets like a tourist was a delight. Left: Dick Likely gets his shoes polished in London, 1943. Below, left: Canadian officers horsing around with kids in the East End of London, 1944. My grandfather is on the far right, wearing the Glengarry. Below, right: Soldiers strolling the High Street in Lincoln, Lincolnshire.

Opposite: Bill MacAskill feeds the pigeons in Trafalgar Square, London, 1945.

Canada House just off Trafalgar Square in London, 1944—then, as now, a home away from home for visiting Canadians.

Above: Big Ben and the Houses of Parliament in London, 1943. Even with air raids, and V1 and V2 rocket attacks, life simply went on as normal for Londoners, who adapted to the privations and inconveniences with good humour and determination. Right: A V2 rocket on display in London. This partial view gives a sense of the power of this silent and deadly German missile. London could easily have been flattened had it not been for Bomber Command's decisive raids on German launch sites on the Continent.

Above: **Canadians going ashore on the southern coast of France, to complete that country's liberation, August 1944. It was a calm landing, as compared with the landings at Normandy in June.**

Opposite, top: **A photograph of the seafront at Dieppe taken by a German photographer around the time of the Canadian raid, August 1942.** Bottom: **The beach at Dieppe where the Canadians landed. The site was a natural killing ground for the Germans positioned on the hills and cliffs overlooking the cobblestone beach; the Canadians never really had a chance. Today, as before the war, this beach is a favourite summer resort, and few traces of the momentous battle remain.**

Left: On the beach at Tel Aviv, Israel, 1942. A ship that carried Jewish refugees seeking a new home in Palestine lies wrecked just off-shore, not far from swimmers. Below: The same beach at Tel Aviv, November 1, 1942.

Opposite, top: Escort destroyers tied up near Murmansk, Russia, 1944. The Russians were dependent on the supply convoys that made this run. Although they were undoubtedly appreciative, when the ships unloaded, the Russians would emerge from their stations, wordlessly take the supplies, and disappear. Opposite, bottom: A Russian destroyer escort awaiting her next run.

On January 3, 1942, Bert Coles was posted to
No. 70 OTU in Nokuru, Kenya, as an instructor.
On the way, he was photographed in front of
the Sphinx in Egypt.

Around the same time, Doug Appleton (centre) and other members of 267 Squadron enjoyed the same sights from a slightly different perspective. These men were all air force, but here they are typical tourists.

Opposite: **Relaxing on the Isle of Capri: Dick Likely (left) and two friends.**

Above: **Padre Laurie Wilmot contemplates the fate of the Christians who died in the Colosseum two thousand years earlier. For Laurie, the time in Rome was a particularly welcome break from battle; he was emotionally and physically drained, having been through a terrible ordeal with the West Novas in an attack in the Liri Valley.** Right: **Mount Vesuvius erupting in March 1944, in a photo taken by RCAF airman Tony Craven.**

Left: A snake charmer near the RAF base in India where RCAF pilot Dick Corbett was posted. Below: Bob Dixon's RCA unit hosts a dinner with residents of an Italian village, 1944. Most Italians were delighted to have the Canadians as their liberators. In some towns, the Italians would cheer the Canadian troops, assuming they were German; when they discovered them to be Canadian, the locals simply adjusted the nationality of their cheers. As with most civilians caught in the crossfire of war, they yearned for life to return to normal.

Opposite: The crew of HMCS *Prince David* unloads supplies and Allied troops on a beautiful beach on Corsica, August 1944.

Opposite: A damaged church in Normandy, 1944.

Above: Spring in Brugge, Belgium, 1945. The beautiful light of this old courtyard, the slender forms of the trees, and the stoic calm of the nun appear timeless and unaffected by war. The courtyard looks the same today.

Above: Canadian liberators and young Dutch women in Holland, 1945. The war wasn't yet over, but the weeks and months of isolation on the front lines were. The Dutch loved the Canadians who freed their country, and it appears here that the Canadians returned their affection.

Opposite, top: American Generals making speeches at the foot of the Arc de Triomphe after the liberation of Paris. General Omar Bradley can be seen in the centre, with the cap and light-coloured tie, just to the right of the base of the street lamp. General de Gaulle purposely stood off camera. Photographer Alex Gray found the French leader to be an arrogant man, with little interest in anything but his return to the capital, and he refused to be photographed with the liberating American forces. Opposite, bottom: Percy Loosemore's RCAPC unit outside the Palais de Versailles in the winter of 1944–45.

Above: The remains of a church in Holland, spring 1945. Normal life was starting to return in the devastated country, but many historic and beautiful buildings were irreparably damaged. Left: Within days of the war's end, there were signs that everyday life was resuming as Dick Field passed through Oldenburg, Germany, on May 6, 1945. Many civilians were very courteous and cooperative, but just as many were silent and avoided eye contact with the occupying Allied forces. The war's end was an uneasy transition for combatants and civilians alike.

The empty streets of Berlin in late May 1945. There was an eerie stillness about the German capital following the demise of the Third Reich. With the encroaching Russian army seeking to grab control of as much of Europe as possible, the Cold War was about to begin.

The Brandenburg Gate in Berlin, as photographed in the rain by my uncle, Bill MacAskill, May 1945. After the war, Berlin was a cold, damp place defined by checkpoints and military police. A package of cigarettes could buy almost anything in the ruined yet hauntingly beautiful city. Many residents had lost everything including any means to earn an income.

Above: American airplanes on display in the plaza below the Eiffel Tower. Dick Likely took this photo from the tower's lowest landing in August 1945. You can get an idea of how high the tower is by how small the planes appear to be below.

Opposite, top: The Eiffel Tower is ghostly through the fog on a rainy day during the time when Parisians were starting to return to something resembling their pre-war lives. Opposite, bottom: Jean-Claude Dubuc (front row, fourth from right) with his regiment, Les Fusiliers Mont-Royal, in Paris, July 1945.

The *Queen Elizabeth* comes into New York harbour in late 1945, bringing thousands of Canadians closer to home. Many servicemen and women waited months in England before finally being assigned a place on board a homeward-bound ship: there simply weren't enough ships.

Opposite: Servicemen take advantage of landing in New York to see some of the sights. Jean-Claude Dubuc (third from left) and friends on top of Rockefeller Center in the fall of 1945.

Archie Byatt and the crew of HMCS *St. Laurent* bury a shipmate on a cold, grey day in Iceland, thousands of miles from family and home.

UNFORGETTABLE AND UNFORGOTTEN

In the early morning hours of August 19, 1942, the Rileys (the Royal Hamilton Light Infantry— RHLI) landed on the beach at Dieppe. The soldiers quickly found themselves trapped in a killing zone, hemmed in by machine gun fire from all sides, and incapacitated by the large round cobblestones that covered the beach and made running impossible, even immobilizing the invading Churchill tanks.

Captain John Foote from Madoc, Ontario, attached himself to the RAP (Regimental Aid Post), which provided only modest cover for the wounded who lay flat on the ground in a slight depression on the rocky shore. Over a period of eight hours, Foote moved up and down the beach tending to the wounded and dying, with no particular regard for his own safety. As the day wore on and escape became impossible for the majority of the soldiers trapped there, Foote refused the chance to retreat to a landing craft and to safety. Instead, he was taken prisoner with thousands of men and spent the remainder of the war in a POW camp, where, during ecumenical services and despite the ever-present albeit uncomprehending German guard, he conveyed regular news of the Allies' progress. In retribution for German losses, many Canadians captured at Dieppe were shackled in irons for almost 18 months and for every Canadian taken prisoner, a French POW was released.

On August 19, the citizens of Dieppe still celebrate what the Canadians did or, as one Frenchman put it, "For giving us hope." They have not forgotten.

Most of the veterans I know feel that their experiences are of small interest, or maybe no one has bothered to remember. But they all carry a story they can't forget. Here are a few of them.

In the summer of 1944, Greg Clark, working as a Canadian war correspondent in Normandy, visited his son on the front line to bring him his favourite lemon meringue pie for his birthday. Alex Gray snapped a picture, no one knowing that a day later Greg's son would be killed.

Jeff Nicklin of the 1st Canadian Parachute Battalion was an ex-Winnipeg Blue Bomber who drove his battalion extremely hard. In response to Jeff's relentless demands, some even protested with a hunger strike. And yet Jeff had trained these men exceptionally well. Nicklin was killed on the airborne assault across the Rhine, and the picture of his simple grave attests to the no-nonsense attitude towards death in war that so many Canadian soldiers personified. When Barney Danson is at any service of remembrance, he thinks of Freddy Harris. John Acheson was on his third bomber mission when they were hit; only John made it out, and he thinks of his crew every day of his life. Jack Hannam, adrift at sea following the tragic sinking of HMCS *Athabascan*, can still recall the bright yellow cap he was wearing that shook a semi-conscious sailor floating in the Atlantic out of his torpor and led to his rescue. Frank Cauley remembers the look on his friend's face as their plane sank with the entire crew trapped on board. Frank, by chance, was next to a raft that deployed when the plane hit the water and broke apart, and was the sole survivor. Howard McNamara's face clouds over as he speaks of the last time he saw his brother James before he was shot down over France. Blackie Blackburn remembers being near the Italian front and giving up his place in the chow line for a DR (dispatch rider) who'd just dropped by, then seeing the chow line hit by German mortars minutes later, killing the DR. Those whose lives were scorched by war never forget.

The war finally over, Percy Loosemore left Holland early one morning to touch base with his unit's HQ at Rheine. He and his driver travelled across the country, finally coming to a long pontoon bridge over the Rhine. Crossing it, they found themselves confronted by a large sign announcing, "You are now entering Germany. No fraternizing."

The guards scrutinized them as they drove slowly past. Percy's driver, Curly, cheerfully chimed up, "So this is Germany…"

It was a desperately long way from Canada, but as they crested a hill, a peaceful scene lay before them, reminding Percy of a time when he was a boy in the south of England.

"I'd climbed to the top of Bury Hill in the South Downs where I stopped and rested, looking down over the peaceful green fields. Years later in Germany, I found myself looking at similar green meadows, a profusion of wildflowers, trees swaying in the breeze with the glint of the sun through their leaves, lazily grazing cattle, and in the distance, some red-bricked dwellings nestling in a shady valley.

"As my eyes turned back to the highway, I couldn't help but visualize those tragic days of 1940 when German tanks sped through here and crashed across the border into Holland, that picturesque and peaceful country we had just left behind. As I continued to admire the beauty of the German countryside, I was utterly at a loss to understand how people dwelling in such a beautiful country could chill their hearts, plunder, destroy and torture other human beings the way they had."

As they crossed back to Belgium, the setting sun cast a warm glow over fields of poppies waving in the evening breeze. Percy could not help but wonder, "Has another generation died in vain?"

The fallen, the friends, the innocents and the lost will always be unforgettable and unforgotten. It's up to us to make sure that their stories pass down to those who don't yet understand.

Jack Harper, rear gunner on Grant McRae's Lancaster, killed in action over Stuttgart, Germany, July 25, 1944.

Im Strand von Dieppe! 19.8.42

Above: Churchill tanks sit stranded in the water on the beach at Dieppe, August 19, 1942. Their treads got jammed with the large, round stones of the beach, and most tanks barely made it off their landing craft.

Opposite: Captured Canadian soldiers are paraded through the streets of Dieppe by German troops now convinced of their invincibility.

Opposite, top: **A Churchill with its tread peeled off.** Opposite, bottom: **Captured Canadians were mistreated on orders from the Führer. They were herded into boxcars, many of them shackled, and transported hundreds of miles to camps, with little food or water during the long trip.**

Above: **Wounded or not, POWs were marched to inland railway terminuses, away from the front and in close groups to deter strafing from Allied aircraft.** Right: **A Canadian cemetery at Dieppe, with a lone biplane flying over in honour.**

Opposite: The church service at Westminster Abbey, taken the morning before Operation Overlord was confirmed as a "go," June 4, 1944.

Above: At Southampton on June 3, 1944, Le Régiment de la Chaudière boards HMCS *Prince David* for the invasion. They were the only Canadians the *Prince David* carried over to Normandy. Left: The second wave of troops leaves HMCS *Prince David* for Juno Beach on June 6, 1944. The men were fired up and champing at the bit to get into action. There had been a delay of twenty-four hours, and they had been cooped up onboard ship for three days. Their war was about to begin.

Left: The grave of 1st Canadian Parachute Battalion commanding officer Jeff Nicklin. Jeff, a lieutenant colonel, was killed by German machine-gun fire as he parachuted in for Operation Varsity, the crossing of the Rhine, March 24, 1945. The Germans expected the invasion, and fighting in the drop zones was heavy. By the end of the first day's action 1,078 men of the 6th Airborne Division had either been killed or wounded; fifty aircraft and eleven gliders were shot down. Below: A 1st Canadian Parachute Battalion paratrooper shows his identification discs to a German officer. The midnight assault on D-Day, undertaken in pitch dark and high winds, was a near disaster. Many paratroopers were killed or taken prisoner, although some achieved tremendous objectives. The same errors would not be made during the assault on the Rhine eight months later.

Right: Sergeant Tommy Prince, MM, First Special Service Force. One of Canada's greatest soldiers. Tom had a rocky time adjusting to civilian life. He died in 1977 at the age of sixty-two, much too young, his wartime achievements nearly forgotten. Below: Casualties in the Ardennes region. On January 2, 1945, the 1st Canadian Parachute Battalion arrived at the front to aid in pushing the Germans out of the Ardennes. The surprise German offensive would come to be known as the Battle of the Bulge. One Canadian paratrooper remembers moving up towards the front line, only to be told by a retreating American soldier, "Hey! Don't go up there—there's Germans!" To which the Canadian replied, "Yeah, we know. That's why we're here."

Life "in the Bag," a phrase used by POWs. Thousands of men spent months or years imprisoned in camps in Germany and Poland. Above: A theatre in Stalag Luft III featured recent hits from London's West End, with costumes and scenery provided by the Germans. Opposite, top: POWs cooking in a camp at the end of the war. After the summer of 1944, Red Cross parcels—the main source of rations for POWs—were all but stopped by the Germans, and food was scarce.

Arthur Thompson from Windsor, Ontario, was working for the Ford Motor Company in Singapore. In 1941, he joined the SSVF (Straits Settlements Volunteer Force), which was attached to the British Army. In February 1942, the British Army in Malaya capitulated to the Japanese invaders. Arthur spent the next three and a half years as a POW first in the horrifically overcrowded Changi Prison (opposite, bottom), then in Thailand and Burma as forced labour building the Thailand-Burma Railway through the Burmese jungle.

An elderly French woman who minutes earlier was practising her English with Alex Gray lies dead after being hit by a flame-thrower. "The problem was she kept running all around the bloody place," Alex recalls. "Some of the guys were getting pretty nervous because of how close the Germans were. She ran around a corner and right into a bloody flame-thrower. Poor old girl; burnt her to a crisp."

Toronto Star correspondent, Greg Clark (cutting pie) had brought a birthday pie to his son, Murray (to Greg's right). The next day, Murray was killed in action and his death devastated Greg. The *Star* wouldn't give Greg leave to grieve with his family, and so he quit the paper. Greg's family didn't see this photograph until 2003, when it was discovered and a copy was sent to them.

On the letter:

FORCES
LETTER

R MAIL

SALVAGED FROM
AIR CRASH.

If anything is enclosed in
this letter it will be sent
by ordinary mail.

Affix
10c or 6d.
Stamp

44

Rec'd
May 15th '44

TO *Lieut R.Y. Likely,*
88th Battery,
5th L.A.A. Reg't, R.C.A.,
(C.A.) C.M.F.

Above: **Dick Likely** with his beloved wife, Helen. When Dick was moving up an Italian mountain with his RCA unit, they stumbled across bushels of letters that had been scattered by a plane that had crashed nearby. Sifting through, one of the soldiers shouted, "Hey, Skip! Here's a letter for you!" Sure enough, it was a letter from Helen that had found its way to Dick by sheer chance. Inset: A photo of Helen's letter to Dick.

Right: Tom and Chris Hare, brothers and RAF pilot friends of Bert Coles. Both men were killed in action.

Above: A graveyard in Italy for soldiers of the Loyal Edmonton Regiment (the Loyal Eddys) killed during the Battle of Ortona, January 7, 1944.

Opposite: German soldiers conducting a *Razzia* (raid) on the streets of Amsterdam, which they did until the final hours of their occupation. This photograph was taken furtively from a second-floor window.

Right: Two Dutch urchins with their prized possession, a tireless bicycle, in Holland, January 1945. Below: French collaborators (some with shaved heads) being held at gunpoint by the Maquis. Alex Gray asked the Resistance members' permission to take pictures, and they cooperatively lined up their captives and made them face the camera. A collaborator's fate was either prison or execution.

Bergen-Belsen concentration camp shortly after it was liberated. Left: An incinerator used to burn corpses. Below: Bunks in a prisoners' barracks.

Opposite: A gallows where inmates were hanged.

Above: Children orphaned at Bergen-Belsen remained in the camp for several months after the war until their futures could be determined.

Opposite: Russian soldiers, prisoners in a concentration camp near Weener, Germany, which was liberated by the Allies, April 24, 1945. Russians released from POW camps faced a harsh welcome in their homeland. A Russian soldier was expected to fight to the death, not surrender. Many returning Russian POWs were interned in gulags in the Soviet Union; some simply "disappeared."

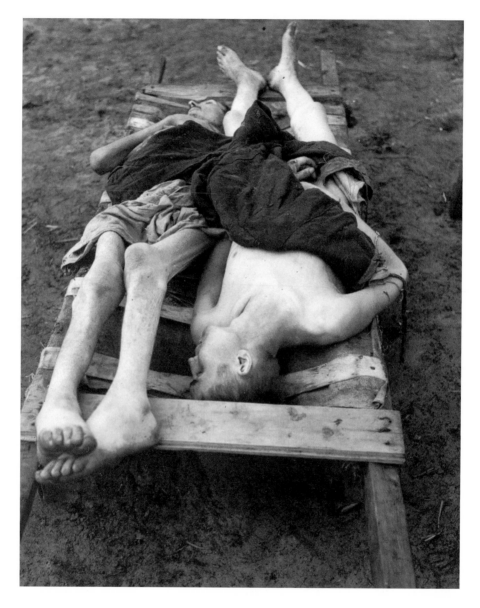

Opposite and above: **Emaciated Russian
soldiers imprisoned at Bergen-Belsen.** Allied
forces who liberated the camps were under
strict instructions not to feed the captives or
even to offer water, because they could die if
they ate or drank substances their systems
could no longer handle. Canadian soldiers
found it painful to keep their distance from
souls so desperately in need.

Opposite, top: **Faded glory. Germans flee Belgium, September 3, 1944. They were without vehicles or fuel, and were reduced to retreating by horse-drawn carts or on foot. This photograph was taken from an upstairs window hours before the liberation of this (unknown) Belgian city.**
Opposite, bottom: **Many paratroopers found themselves in Wismar, Germany, at the end of the war. Here, a paratrooper has spread out on a table a Nazi flag, a treasured souvenir of victory.**

Above: **Unlike the SS or the Hitler Youth, older, weary German troops were relieved to see the war end and happy to return to their homes and families in one piece.**

Opposite: Devastation in Berlin, May 1945, a broken city just weeks after Hitler's suicide. His bunker was beneath the rubble at the extreme right of the picture.

Above: The Tomb of the Unknown Soldier in Paris, 1945. As in Ottawa, Arlington, and Westminster Abbey, this memorial was created to honour those men and women, be they navy, army, air force, or merchant marine, who died for their country. For the families of the millions of soldiers of all wars whose remains were never found, the Tomb of the Unknown Soldier provides a place of closure for the fallen, both unforgettable and unforgotten.

1st Canadian Parachute Battalion members take a last look at a sign and flag at their camp at Bulford, in Wiltshire. The war had just ended, and the paratroopers were soon to be shipped home from England.

LONG LIVE CANADA

MAPLE LEAF UP

The phrase "Maple Leaf Up" was used on signs that were posted along the road leading to the Canadian front. This was the logistics lifeline that extended from the Normandy beaches through France and deep into the Low Countries of the Netherlands. Along this line travelled thousands of CMP (Canadian Military Pattern) trucks bearing cargos of food, ammunition, weapons and reinforcements. On the return from the front, the route was marked "Maple Leaf Down," and it was a route for the wounded and for those who'd been relieved.

From being a largely agricultural nation, Canada went through a massive industrial change to rise to the demands of war. The fighting force of the First Canadian Army was predominantly comprised of volunteer troops—rare among the nations engaged in World War II.

Young men and women from across the country escaped unemployment, the confines of small town life, boredom, school, limited prospects, financial straits, and even privilege, to step into a demanding world of routine and discipline. In the service, they learned to get the job done, whether that meant walking into enemy fire or holystoning a ship's deck.

One tactic Canadians learned in battle was to take the most difficult route. The reasoning was simple: if you took the easy way, that's where the enemy would likely lie in wait. But if you took the rough road and slogged it out, the hard work could pay off mightily.

As Jack Granatstein has noted, "There was scarcely a family in the land that did not have someone in the service," and this helped forge a unanimity within the service with few discipline problems and deep bonds of kinship. It also refined the ability to keep driving forward, regardless of setbacks. This determination was a great source of pride among the ranks. In 1944, the Canadians returned to Dieppe, the scene of the disastrous raid two years earlier; they also returned to Vimy Ridge, a site synonymous with one of the great victories of World War I; and in the final months of that year, they pressed on into the Netherlands, the final drive to oust the Nazis as they'd done in Italy, in the North Atlantic, and in the air.

To a world at war, "Maple Leaf Up" was a sign, both literally and figuratively, that liberation was at hand. Percy Loosemore remembers a trip in May 1945.

"When we entered Holland from Belgium, the Dutch people seemed overwhelmed with joy at their deliverance and the end of the war; for while the Belgians had been liberated for some time, the Dutch were celebrating both the end of the war in Europe and their own immediate liberation. Bunting hung everywhere; people cheered as we drove by; children waved Dutch red, white and blue flags; and crowds gathered in anticipation of victory parades, so that we often had to detour around the centre of a town. Once, when I stopped my car, children gathered around and proceeded to decorate our vehicle with flowers and coloured streamers. To witness the enthusiastic joy and happy faces of these people was a greater pleasure to me than to be amongst the cheering crowds in London, Paris, or New York. I was deeply moved."

And yet for all of their victories and accomplishments, the celebrations and enthusiastic receptions, the only thing our veterans wanted was the chance to get back to Canada and to start living in peace again.

As the troopships drew into Halifax harbour and Pier 21 came into view, even the weariest and hardest of hearts warmed to the thought that "Maple Leaf Up" now meant that the road home had reached its end.

Opposite, top: **Troops marching down Government Street in Victoria, 1941, on their way to Canada's east coast and from there to England. This is the same route that veterans march on their way to the Cenotaph every Remembrance Day.** Opposite, bottom: **The first contingent of CWACs march with pride in British Columbia, 1942. They had only recently been issued uniforms, although they'd been training for some months.**

Below: **Navigation training with bubble sextants at Pennfield Ridge, New Brunswick, September 1941. Taking celestial readings to determine location was standard procedure for RCAF navigators and was used throughout the war.**

Overleaf: **The first contingent of Canadian-born Chinese soldiers in Wetaskiwin, Alberta. After years of trying, these young men were finally accepted into the service, many joining the SOE's Force 136. Herb Lim was one of the distinguished number of Chinese-Canadian special-force soldiers who saw action in India and Burma.**

Opposite: Charles Phelan, Royal Canadian Horse Artillery, at Lamone River, Italy, February 1945. Charles was trapped in France when Germany invaded in 1940, but he managed to escape back to the UK in the nick of time.

Above: Dick Likely (centre) on the road northwards in Italy in 1943. Dick is holding a photograph of his wife, Helen, whom he had married before he shipped out overseas.

Above: Dick Likely, age 21, at the OTC (Officers' Training Camp) in Brockville, Ontario. Eventually renamed No. 1 Officers' Training Centre, by 1945 it had graduated more than ten thousand junior army officers. Its motto was *Qui nocent docent* ("Those who can harm can teach").

Opposite: A paratrooper of the 1st Canadian Parachute Battalion advancing in an open field at Bulford during a training exercise, December 1943. The paratroopers' wartime commander, James Hill, recalls: "During the physical training we focused on four objectives: speed, control, simplicity and fire effect. To achieve [this], we had to become amazingly fit. The initial training was extremely hard, and many volunteers left—they simply couldn't stand the pace."

Left: Pilot Officer John "Scruffy" Weir of 401 Squadron, 1941. John was shot down during a sweep of Normandy, while trying to "nurse-maid" a Sprog pilot who was killed in action. John ended up in Stalag Luft III, where he played an integral role in the "Great Escape."

Below: Flight Officer E.L. Neal, Pilot Officer Ian Ormston (right), RCAF pilots with 401 Squadron seconded to the RAF, flying Hurricanes and Spitfires. "Ormy" was on the sweep with Scruffy and saw him shot down. They remain close friends to this day.

Opposite: Vern Williams, a navigator on a Mosquito, in a photograph taken for fake ID cards to be used in the event of being shot down over enemy territory.

Life "on the line" with the Royal Canadian
Artillery during the Italian campaign, 1944.

A Canadian soldier reading a newspaper
during a lull in the Battle of Ortona.

Opposite: War artist Lawren Harris Jr., son of Group of Seven member Lawren Harris, in Italy, 1944. Lawren worked extensively with my grandfather as one of Canada's war artists.

Right: A seaman proudly chalks up his ship's first kill on the stack of HMCS *Chaudière* which, along with the *Ottawa* and the *Kootenay*, was responsible for sinking two German U-boats, August 21, 1944. Below: Gerry Wall, on anti-aircraft watch during King George IV's visit to HMCS *Sioux* at Scapa Flow. Located in the Orkney Islands off the northeast coast of Scotland, this historic stretch of water played an important role during both world wars.

Above: Jim Jones of the Sherbrooke Fusiliers in Grave, Holland, December 1944. The Allied armies dug in to holding positions for several frigid winter months before the final drive to Berlin resumed in February 1945. Note the extra armour—recycled tank treads—welded to the tank for protection against the German 88s' deadly armour-piercing shells.

Opposite: Canadian soldiers emerge from a small tunnel on the north side of Ortona during the battle for that Italian city.

Above: **A *Windsor Star* luncheon reunion in Piccadilly, June 29, 1943. From the left: Douglas MacFarlane, Peter MacRitchie, Burton G. Johnston, Harold M. Morden, Eric Gibbs, and Jack Dalgleish.**

Clockwise from top left: **Douglas MacFarlane, editor of *The Maple Leaf* and one of the great Canadian war correspondents, writing in the field in France, 1944; Pierre Faribault, in the south of England in September 1944, the week before going over to the Continent with Les Fusiliers Mont-Royal. Joe King, 1st Canadian Parachute Battalion, on a dispatch rider's motorcycle, Germany, 1945; Major Eric Heathcote, London, 1945.**

Above: Canadian graves on the road through Holland. Temporary gravesites such as this were scattered across the country and were a sobering sight to Allied troops liberating the Netherlands.

Opposite, top: Paratroopers from the 1st Canadian Parachute Battalion resting before a river crossing that would take them one step closer to Germany and to returning home. Bottom: Beginning with Operation Varsity, the 1st Canadian Parachute Battalion raced across Belgium and then north to Wismar, Germany, where they drew a line in the sand against advancing Russian troops.

Clem Pearce joined the RCAF seeking to avenge the death of his brother, Basil, who was killed in action. Clem enlisted as an air gunner, was shot down, and survived the long winter march from the POW camps to Lübeck, Germany.

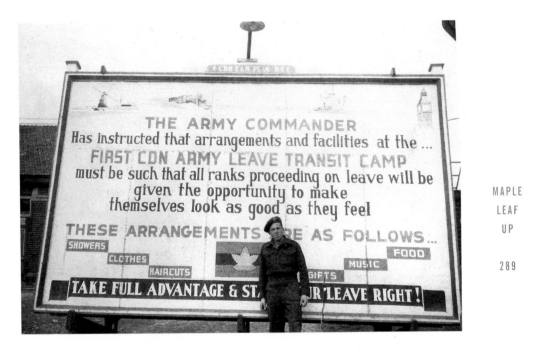

THE ARMY COMMANDER
Has instructed that arrangements and facilities at the ...
FIRST CDN ARMY LEAVE TRANSIT CAMP
must be such that all ranks proceeding on leave will be
given the opportunity to make
themselves look as good as they feel

THESE ARRANGEMENTS ARE AS FOLLOWS...
SHOWERS
CLOTHES
HAIRCUTS
FOOD
MUSIC
GIFTS
TAKE FULL ADVANTAGE & ST... UR LEAVE RIGHT!

Engineer Morden Walker standing in front of a sign for the 1st Canadian Army Leave Transit Camp. The logistical challenges of keeping an army of hundreds of thousands of servicemen and women fed, clothed and clean were daunting. Leave centres gave service members a chance to refresh themselves before heading out on leave. Captain Charles Scot-Brown, CANLOAN, recalls, "The fighting soldier's greatest thrill was having a bath and being able to sit down in peace and quiet with a nice hot meal. The simple things were what you wanted."

Left: Canadian soldiers delousing Russian POWs liberated from concentration camps, May 1945. Below: Queen Elizabeth, wife of King George VI, inspects Canadian women serving at 6 Bomber Group HQ in Yorkshire, 1945.

Opposite: Lieutenant J. Kostelac of Calgary showing the US/Canada shoulder-sleeve insignia worn by all members of the First Special Service Force, an elite force of Canadian and American soldiers whose exploits were legendary. On March 4, 1944, Kostelac went missing in action and is presumed dead.

Opposite: **Abandoned motorcycles and weapons stretching as far as the eye can see. Melancholy sights like this were common across the Continent when the war ended; virtually all the weapons were sold as scrap.**

Above: **Germans surrendering their weapons to Canadian forces in Holland, May 1945.**

Overleaf: **The ghost town of Arnhem, the Netherlands, in 1945. The "Maple Leaf Up" sign directs traffic north towards the Canadian front line.**

Above: A Canadian liberator is enthusiastically welcomed by Dutch women, 1945.

Opposite: When Alex Gray found himself in Lille, after the liberation of France, his jeep was swarmed with people. He was taken into a wine merchant's cellar, where his vehicle was filled with bottles of champagne, which he took back to the war correspondents' camp. The wine went so fast that he was lucky to save one bottle for himself.

Overleaf, left: The Sherbrooke Fusiliers roll through Xanten, Germany, on their return to the Netherlands following the unconditional German surrender, May 1945. Right: Dutch citizens celebrate the arrival of Canadian troops in Amsterdam after liberation.

Left: A 1st Canadian Parachute Battalion corporal has a chat with a toddler at his own level.

Below: Percy Loosemore photographed the Canadians liberating Brugge, Belgium, in September 1944. The blurred action in the picture effectively captures the energetic spirit of the day.

Atop his Sherman tank, a Sherbrooke Fusilier is effusively welcomed in Holland in the spring of 1945. The Dutch wanted to shake hands, plant kisses, pinch cheeks, or just touch the Canadians who brought freedom with them.

In the Far East, the war continued throughout the summer of 1945. In this photograph, Herb Lim of SOE Force 136 strikes a pose worthy of his special-operations training and his defiance towards the enemy. The members of Force 136 were well aware that should they be captured, they would be summarily executed as spies.

Marcel Croteau is awarded the Distinguished Flying Cross by King George VI, a singular honour for an air gunner. Even today, Marcel still shows the focus and determination that earned him the DFC.

Above: On board a ship sailing home, this artillery soldier watches a "liberty ship" passing the other way without the fear of a U-boat attack. Left: Hanging over the railing of the *Queen Elizabeth* as she is eased into Halifax harbour, and as the men get their first glimpse of Pier 21.

Opposite: Captain Armstrong, RCAPC, taking the air onboard the *Queen Elizabeth*, bound for Canada, 1946.

Overleaf, left: On the dock in Halifax, June 1945. Three of the men in this picture were POWs who had shared the same room at Stalag Luft III. (Right to left) John Colwell, Art Hawtin, Ken Banks, John Acheson, and an unidentified airman. Right: The 1st Canadian Parachute Battalion preparing to march up University Avenue upon their return to Toronto in late June 1945. They had been brought back early to prepare to head off to the Pacific after a month's leave, but the war's end kept them in Canada.

A temporary graveyard in Holland, 1945. Great pains were taken to identify properly the name, unit, and location of the remains of every fallen soldier, which were eventually transferred to one of the hundreds of Commonwealth War Graves.

CHRONOLOGY

3 Sep 1939	Britain declares war
10 Sep 1939	Canada declares war
6 Oct 1939	Hitler proposes peace with Britain and France in return for recognition of status quo; both countries reject this.
8 Apr 1940	British Commonwealth Air Training Plan opens No. 1 ITS at the Eglinton Hunt Club, Toronto
9 Apr 1940	Hitler invades Norway and Denmark
10 May 1940	Hitler invades the Low Countries and France
15 May 1940	Netherlands surrenders
23 May 1940	Canadian 1st Division ordered to France to secure Dunkirk perimeter. Canadian 1st Division reaches France
24 May 1940	Bismark sinks HMS *Hood*
25 May 1940	Operation Dynamo: the evacuation of the BEF at Dunkirk begins
26 May 1940	Bismark sunk
8 Jun 1940	Canadian 1st Division moves into France as a Second British Expeditionary Force
10 Jun 1940	Italy enters war
13 Jun 1940	Canadian 1st Division evacuated from Brittany
14 Jun 1940	Paris falls to the Germans

14 June 1940	A site near Victoria, Newfoundland, is chosen for a POW camp
July 1940	A camp is established at Gravenhurst, Ontario, for German POWs (35,000 German POWs received during the War by Canadian camps)
10 Jul 1940	Luftwaffe bombing of Welsh ports inaugurates the Battle of Britain
26 Aug 1940	First engagement, over south England, between an RCAF squadron and the Luftwaffe
31 Aug 1940	Operation Sea Lion in planning: German successes against the RAF incite Hitler to schedule a land invasion of Britain for September 21
7 Sep 1940	The Blitz begins
17 Sep 1940	Hitler postpones Sea Lion indefinitely
27 Sep 1940	Germany, Italy and Japan sign tripartite pact in Berlin
14 Nov 1940	Luftwaffe firebombing of Coventry
13 Apr 1941	Germany invades Russia
10 May 1941	Last night of the Blitz and the Luftwaffe's heaviest attack on a British city
1 August 1941	Camp X, SOE, goes into operation in Whitby, Ontario, to train special agents for secret overseas operations
7 Nov 1941	Canadians land in Hong Kong to reinforce British
7 Dec 1941	Japanese bomb Pearl Harbour
11 Dec 1941	Winnipeg Grenadiers reinforce Gin Drinkers' Line on Chinese Mainland
18 Dec 1941	Japanese land on island of Hong Kong
25 Dec 1941	Hong Kong falls to Japanese
14 Jan 1942	Canadian government orders the evacuation of all male Japanese nationals to the interior. (Those resisting evacuation were sent to a camp in Angler, Ontario, on Lake Superior)
1 Feb 1942	German U-boats adopt Enigma code machine
24 April 1942	Conscription plebiscite called by Mackenzie King
11 May 1942	Canadian Parliament passes bill for the introduction of full conscription
27 April 1942	Canadians vote for conscription (3 to 1) in plebiscite
11 May 1942	Parliament passes bill for introduction of full military conscription
19 Aug 1942	Operation Jubilee: Assault on Dieppe by a predominantly Canadian force
Oct 1942	Government sets up 8 camps for Japanese in the interior of British Columbia. (In all, 22,000 people of Japanese descent sent to internment camps)
9 Oct 1942	U-69 attacks a freighter in the St-Lawrence estuary 173 miles from Quebec City
10 Jul 1943	Canadians land at Pacino Beach, Sicily
15 Aug 1943	First Special Service Force, including 5,300 Canadians, lands on Kiska in the Aleutians

3 Sep 1943	1st Canadian division lands on Italian mainland and captures Reggio di Calabria
28 Dec 1943	Canadians capture Ortona
24 Mar 1944	"The Great Escape" from Stalag Luft III
11 May 1944	Canadian armor supports allied attacks on the Gustav line and Monte Cassino
23 May 1944	1st Canadian Corps breaks the Hitler Line; advances up Liri Valley
4 Jun 1944	Rome liberated
6 Jun 1944	Operation Overlord: Allies land in Normandy on D-Day; 1st Canadian Parachute Battalion dropped after midnight; 3rd Canadian Infantry lands at Juno Beach
10 Jul 1944	Canadians capture Caen
25 Jul 1944	Canadians capture Verrières Ridge in Normandy; Black Watch suffers heavy casualties
7 Aug 1944	Operation Totalize: Canadians mount an operation to close the Falaise Gap
21 Aug 1944	Falaise Gap successfully closed, but 30,000 Germans escape
25 Aug 1944	Paris liberated
30 Aug 1944	Two Canadian brigades break the Gothic Line
1 Sep 1944	2nd Canadian Infantry Division captures Dieppe
17 Sep 1944	In the Netherlands Operation Market Garden begins
21 Sep 1944	Gothic Line completely collapses; Canadians enter Rimini
30 Sep 1944	Canadian 3rd Division captures Calais
1 Oct 1944	Canadian 2nd Division begins Scheldt offensive, to open port of Antwerp
14 Oct 1944	Canadian ships land Greek and British troops to Piraeus, Greece
31 Oct 1944	South Beveland peninsula falls to Canadians
28 Nov 1944	First Allied convoy disembarks at port of Antwerp
16 Dec 1944	Battle of the Bulge, the last German offensive in the west, begins
8 Feb 1945	Operation Veritable launched towards Rhine
21 Feb 1945	Canadian and British "water rats" break Siegfried Line
23 Mar 1945	Operation Plunder: Canadians cross the Rhine near Wesel
15 Apr 1945	Canadians take Arnhem
16 Apr 1945	Canadians liberate Groningen
5 May 1945	German troops in Netherlands surrender to General Foulkes
8 May 1945	VE Day
31 May 1945	Camp X closes
6 Aug 1945	Americans drop atom bomb on Hiroshima; Nagasaki targeted on 9 August
14 Aug 1945	VJ Day

311

VETERANS INTERVIEWED

George Abbas	Dick Bartlett	Herb Boake
John Acheson	Leopold Beauchamp	George Borgal
Alice Adams	Brenda Beech	Frank Boyd
Andy Anderson	Jake Beer	Bob Boyle
John Anderson	Jack Bennett	Elizabeth Breckenridge
Tom Anstey	James Bennett	John Breckenridge
Doug Appleton	Paul Benson	Dale Brecknell
David Arksey	Rodrigue Berger	Ray Briggs
Hilda Ashwell	Keith Besley	Peter Briscoe
Sheridan Atkinson	Stanley Biggs	Antonio Brisebois
Elizabeth Audley-Charles	Jim Birrell	Frank Britten
Ray Baines	Arthur Bishop	Michael Brodsky
Bill Baker	Blackie Blackburn	Cecil Brooks
Herbert Baldwin	George Blackburn	Clarence Brown
St. Clair Balfour	Gérald Blackett	Forbes Brown
Russell Bannock	John Blakelock	Keith Brown
David Barker	Doug Blakely	Jim Brownell
Mel Barrett	Woodrow Blakely	Bob Buchanan

Ernest Burchell	Jack Clements	Kenneth Curry
John Burgess	Mabel Clements	Jean Marcel D'Aoust
Russ Burrows	Al Clevette	Horace (Monty) Dabbs
Ron Butcher	Ivor Cobb	Robert Dale
Veronica Butcher	Jack Cockrell	Norman Daly
Nancy Butler	Jim Coffey	Barney Danson
Archie Byatt	Bert Coles	Guy Dartois
Hudson Byers	Bob Collins	Bob Davis
George Campbell	Alex Colville	Jack Davis
James R. Campbell	John Colwell	T.G. (Gerry) Davis
Les Canivet	Bill Cook	Joan de Bustin
Ione Canning	Lionel Cook	Jan de Vries
Goldie Cantor	Nora Cook	Rod Deon
Saul Cantor	John Cooper	Leonard Desjarlais
George Carlow	Howie Copeman	Richard Dillon
James Carrington	Dick Corbett	John Dix
Clive Caswell	Donald Cornell	Bob Dixon
Les Cater	Jack Corrie	Bud Donnelly
Frank Cauley	Geoffrey Corry	Lloyd Dopson
Paul Chan	Geoff Costeloe	Jean-Claude Dubuc
Peter Chance	Ernest Coté	Lou Duffley
William Charlton	Marc Coupal	Phyllis Dufton
Don Cheney	Merv Couse	Barb Duncan
Bruce Chisholm	Tony Cowling	Hunter Dunn
Stephen Chisholm	Norman Cox	Derek Eckersely
Jacques Chouinard	Walter Cox	Tom Eckford
Vince Clair	Tony Craven	Stocky Edwards
Irene Clark	Stan Croft	Don Elliott
John Clark	Marcel Croteau	Arnott England

Peter Fairclough

Pierre Faribault

James Ferster

Dick Field

Jim Finnie

Michael Finnis

Bob Firlotte

Victor Flett

John Flinn

Dennis Flynn

Charles Forbes

Roy Forsey

Barbara Fosdick

314 Bob Foster

Andy Foulds

Fred Fowlow

Charles Fox

Harry Fox

Donald Francis

Bob Furneaux

Mary Galbraith

Jack Gallagher

Strome Galloway

Glenn Gardiner

Pierre Gauthier

Beatrice Geary

Joe Gelleny

Lloyd George

Harold Ghent

Harry Gibson

Tom Gilday

Patricia Gill

Gerald Goddard

Louis Godin

Eddie Goodman

John Gorsline

Clément Gosselin

Jack Gouinlock

Bonnie Joan Graham

Kit Graham

William Graham

Bob Grant

Kurt Grant

Alex Gray

Bill Grierson

Tony Griffin

Joe Griffith

D.W. Griffiths

Bob Grogan

Victor Guérin

Ed Haddon

Bob Haden

Margaret Haliburton

Julie Hallett

Jack Hannam

Ray Hardick

Reg Harrison

David Lloyd Hart

Harold (Red) Hayes

E.T.B. Heathcote

Fred Heather

Pauline Hebb

Richard Heward

Allan Hilborn

Dick Hilborn

Werner Hirschmann

Roy Hogan

Gordon Hogarth

Orille Hogue

Doris Hope

Steve Horan

Don Horne

William Howe

Harry Humphries

Harold (Hutch) Hutchinson

Tom Ingham

Andy Irwin

Georges Isabelle

Rolph Jackson

W.S. (Bill) Jackson

Joe Jamieson

Alex Jardine

Henryk Jedwab

Bill Jenkins

Arthur Johnston

Peter Johnston

Gwilym Jones

Jim Jones

Mervin Jones

Phyllis Jones

William Joyce

Vic Karpinski

Ken Keegan

Gerry Keeler

Jeff Kelly

Jim Kelly

Irene Kendrew

Gil Kenny

James Kenny

Roy Kent

Jack Kerr

Peter Kerr

Arthur Kinnis

Roland Lafontaine

Gilles Lamontagne

Fred Lamourea

Barbara (Reg) Lane

Tom Lane

Vickie Laprairie

Roger LaRocque

Lucien Lavoie

C. E. Law

Alan Lawrence

Norman Lawrence

Tom Lawrence

Albert LeBlanc

Léon LeBlanc

Charles Lepine

John Leprich

Elsa Lessard

Gerald Levenston

Mike Lewis

Dick Likely

Herb Lim

John Lipton

Cecil Litster

Tony Little

Stanley Livingston

Percy Loosemore

Merv Loucks

Wally Loucks

William Loucks

James Low

Vera Low

Finn Lunde

Don Lush

Michael Lustgarten

O. J. (Dusty) Lutes

Norbert Luth

Sigmond Lysek

William MacAskill

Bill MacDonald

Doug MacDonald

Lloyd MacDonald

Wally Mace

Russ Macfarlane

Alex MacInnis

Don MacIntyre

Jack Mackenzie

Ian MacKinnon

Jack MacKinnon

Roger MacLellan

Bob Madill

William Magee

Geoffrey Marlow

John Marsh

Bob Marshall

Jack Martin

Red Martin

Joseph A. Maruca

Gord Marwick

Bill Mason

Chuck Mawer

Martin Maxwell

Jim McCague

Tom McCusker

Germain McDuff

Don McGregor

Bernice McIntyre

Harold (Corky) McKay

Mark McKinney

Anne McNamara

Howard McNamara

Grant McRae

Carl McVicar	E. R. Pellant	MacGregor Roulston
Bruce Medd	Florence Pennington	Bill Royds
Martin Meech	Herb Peppard	Frank Rusling
Raymond Meloche	Bruno Petrenko	Bob Rutherford
Bob Middlemass	C.D. Phelan	Arthur Sager
Paul Mimeault	Desmond Piers	Frank Saies-Jones
George Moncton	William Pippy	Harry Saring
Don Montgomery	Frank Planes	Jim Saunders
Basil H. (Pat) Moore	Gordon M. Platt	Stu Saunders
Hilda Moore	Fred Pollak	Harry Schmuck
Ken Moore	Bob Porter	Heinz Scholz
Lee Morgan	Jim Potter	Charles Scot-Brown
Don Morrison	Paul-Émile Pouliot	Barbara Scott
Fernand Mousseau	Ralph Punt	Ron Searle
Ruth Muggeridge	Gordie Quan	Fred H. Seeley
Bob Mullin	Wilf Quinn	Clou Sévigny
Bill Needles	S.V. Radley-Walters	Pierre Sévigny
Jack Nelles	Roland Reid	Meyer Shear
Ken Ney	Keith Reynolds	George Shearman
Pat Nixon	Jack Rice	Brian Shelley
Elizabeth Orford	Marcel Richard	Ray Sherk
Ian Ormston	Léon Rioux	Lorne Shetler
Joe Ouellette	Bill Ritchie	W.E. Chick Sills
Nancy Page	Emlyn Roberts	Edward Simpson
Lou Pantaleo	Lloyd Robertson	Jack Simpson
Ric Parker	Guy Robitaille	Britton Smith
Bill Paton	Richard Rohmer	David Smith
Chris Patton	Joseph Romanow	Don Smith
Clem Pearce	Charles (Bud) Roos	Eric Smith

316

Wally Smythe

Frank Snary

Jack Southern

Lawrence Spinks

Jack Staley

Pete Stanger

Bill Stephenson

Jim Stephenson

Bill Stevens

Kay Stevens

R. V. Stevenson

Neil Stewart

Raymond Stoker

Daureen Stover

John Stroud

Don Sutherland

Larry Sutherland

Henri Tellier

Joan Thomas

Mary Thomas

John Thompson

Alex Thorpe

Tom Treherne

Fernand Trépanier

Maurice Tugwell

Gilles Turcot

Bill Turnell

Merv Utas

Saunders Valensky

George Vant Haaf

Patricia Vant Haaf

Fred Vincent

Bill Waddell

William Waddell

Tom Wagner

Max Walker

Morden Walker

Al Wallace

Art Wallace

Les Wallace

Nita Walt

Stanley Wardill

Reg Watt

Garth Webb

Reg Weeks

John Weicker

John Weir

Denis Whitaker

Vern White

Bill Wickens

Bob Wight

Lloyd Wigmore

John Wilkes

Owen Williams

Vern Williams

Harvey Willis

Laurie Wilmot

Gerry Wilson

Hill Wilson

Ralph Wilson

Norm Wilton

Tony Winstanley

Victor Wong

Bill Wonnacott

Karl Work

Peter Worthington

Cyril Yarnell

Malcolm Young

Philip Young

Art Younger

ACKNOWLEDGEMENTS

My first debt of gratitude is to all those who have been interviewed for the Testaments of Honour project, and those who are yet to come. A complete list of those interviewed at the date of printing can be found beginning on page 312.

The project has taken seven years to date, greatly facilitated by the support of George Weston Limited, the Department of Canadian Heritage, Veterans Affairs Canada and the Canada Remembers Heroes Remember initiative, Alberta Energy Company Ltd., Harrison McCain Foundation, Ontario Trillium Foundation, Alliance Atlantis/History Television, Caldwell Securities, Carolyn Sifton Foundation, Charles H. Ivey Foundation, Fairmont Hotels & Resorts, CN, Donner Canadian Foundation, F. K. Morrow Foundation, Homestead Land Holdings Ltd., Hydro One Inc., J.P. Bickell Foundation, JVC Canada, @Last Software, Manulife Financial, McLean Foundation, Precision Camera Inc., Richard Ivey Foundation, Rothmans Inc., Musonic Ltd., Royal Bank Financial Group Foundation, Royal Canadian Legion Branches 264, 284, 291, and 292, the Royal Canadian Naval Association (Victoria Branch), The Jackman Foundation, The Norman and Margaret Jewison Charitable Foundation, and The Queen's Own Rifles of Canada.

In no lesser degree, many friends and veterans have helped the Project's work with financial support, including Barbara and Blake Heathcote, Walter Hanbidge, Don McGregor, Garfield Mitchell, Archie Byatt, Bob Grant, Ric Parker, John B. Wilkes, St. Clair Balfour, John Weir, Nora Cook, John Acheson, Gordon Hogarth, Bill Jackson, John Gorsline, Britt Smith, Robert Dale,

Wally Loucks, Philip and Ann Foster, James Kenny, David Barker, Donald Sutherland, Peter Briscoe, John Matthews, Bob Haden, Jan Goddard, Christine Pickios, Gordie Quan, Dick Likely, Florence Pennington, Doug Appleton, Rolph Jackson, Cy Yarnell, Morden Walker, Jim Birrell, Art Wallace, Jack Nelles, Ken Moore, Jim Coffey, Arthur Johnston, Roger MacLellan, John Marsh, Andrew Foulds, Barbara Fosdick, Nita Walt, and Jack Kerr. I hope that anyone who has inadvertently been missed in this list will forgive me.

The support of the publishers and editors at Doubleday Canada has been extraordinary, and I am most indebted for the friendship and support of Martha Kanya-Forstner, Susan Burns, Brad Martin, Scott Richardson, Stephanie Gowan, and Maya Mavjee.

Numerous individuals, in addition to the generosity of the veterans and their families, have been instrumental in facilitating the work of the Testaments of Honour Historical Archive. They include my great friend and sounding board Danylo Dzwonyk, Major-General Lewis MacKenzie, Roy Whitsed, Matt and Dolf Grosfeld, Ed Brecknell, Alex Colville, Jenny Chesson, Jack and Dawn Burgess, Bruce Burgess, Bob Hawkes, Ron Chisholm (MLA Nova Scotia), Bert Coles, Siobhain Fray, Nick McGrath, Bob D'Avignon, Jacob Barker, Captain Stephen Roberts, Bill Stern, Walter Levitt, Sherida Caldwell, Richard MacFarlane, Louise Côté and Sandra Duchesne (and staff) at Ste-Anne-de-Bellevue, Donna Serra of PWGSC, General Paul Manson (ret'd), Bill Wilson and the Naval Museum of Alberta, Emery Lalonde, Mark Laurie for his exemplary research, Maurice Dessureault, Yves Falardeau for his assistance with the Francophone interviews, Donal Foley for his dedication, insight, and friendship, Jan de Vries and the 1st Canadian Parachute Battalion Association for their great support, Barbara Duncan who has worked tirelessly for the project, and Barbara Heathcote, my mother, for her endless encouragement and contributions. I'm most fortunate for the patience and support of my wife Ellen Hanbidge and my daughters Elisabeth and Maggie: thank you all, with much love.

Finally, without the friendship, energy, advice and inspiration of Major-General Pierre Lalonde (ret'd), the continued work of Testaments of Honour would have been impossible; my debt to him is incalculable. Thank you, Pierre.

PHOTO CREDITS

All photographs, except those marked with an (*), are from the Testaments of Honour Historical Archive collection. They have come from the following individuals and sources. Every attempt has been made to provide correct and appropriate credit. Major E.T. Heathcote MM ED, 2IC of the Canadian Army's Historical Unit owned a substantial collection of images, some of which may be found in secondary sources. Inquiries for use of any of the photographs in this volume should be directed to Testaments of Honour, www.testaments.ca.

GENERAL PHOTOS
Endpapers, E.T. Heathcote; Cover, E.T. Heathcote; i, Nora Cook; ii, Doug Appleton; iii, Bert Coles; iv, Forbes Brown; v, Jean-Claude Dubuc; vi, Fred Pollak; vii, E.T. Heathcote; viii–ix, E.T. Heathcote; xii, John Gorsline; xiv, Dick Likely; xvi, E.T. Heathcote; 5, Dubuc

ON THE ROAD
6–7, 1st Canadian Parachute Battalion; 10, E.T. Heathcote; 11, Vickie LaPrairie; 12, R.V. Stevenson; 13, Wally Loucks; 14, Top L, Tom Ingham; Top R, Marcel Croteau; Bottom L, Joe Jamieson; Bottom R, Alex Jardine; 15, Top L, Art Wallace; Top R, Leopold Beauchamp; Bottom, E.T. Heathcote; 16, Top, L, Dusty Lutes; Top R, Doug Appleton; Bottom, Anne McNamara; 17, Doug Appleton; 18, Dale Brecknell; 19, Victor Wong; 20, Trixie Geary; 21, Top, Dusty Lutes; Bottom, E.T. Heathcote; 22, Doug Appleton; 22, Top, Doug Appleton; Bottom, John Gorsline; 23, Top L, Doug Appleton; R and Bottom, Dick Likely; 24, 1st Canadian Parachute Battalion; 25, Top, Alex Gray; Bottom, Joan Thomas; 26, Top, Dick Field; Bottom, Doug Appleton; 27, June McRae; 28–29, Mel

Barrett; 30–31 Alex Gray; 32, Top, Alex Gray; Bottom, E.T. Heathcote; 33, Jim Jones; 34, E.T. Heathcote; 35, Alex Gray; 36, Top, Percy Loosemore; Bottom L, Alex Gray; Bottom R, Dick Likely; 37, Alex Gray; 38, Jim Jones; 39, 1st Canadian Parachute Battalion; Top L, Fred Pollak; Top R, Nora Cook; Bottom, Maurice Tugwell; 41, Top L, Maurice Tugwell; Top R, Alex Gray; Bottom, 1st Canadian Parachute Battalion; 42, Top, Jim Jones; Bottom, Percy Loosemore; 43, 1st Canadian Parachute Battalion; 44–45, Percy Loosemore; 46, Top, 1st Canadian Parachute Battalion; Bottom, E.T. Heathcote; 47, Percy Loosemore

COMING OF AGE
48–49, Barbara Duncan; 52, Barbara Duncan; 53, James Campbell; 54, Top L, Irene Kendrew; Top R, Elizabeth Orford; Bottom, Trixie Geary; 55, Vickie LaPrairie; 56–57, Victor Wong; 58, Joan Thomas; 59, Top L, Ione Canning; Top R, Percy Loosemore; Bottom, 1st Canadian Parachute Battalion; 60, Top L, 1st Canadian Parachute Battalion; Top R, Pierre Faribault; Bottom, 1st Canadian Parachute Battalion; 61, 1st Canadian Parachute Battalion; 62, Top, Pierre Faribault; Bottom, Dick Likely; 63, Nita Walt; 64, Top, Pierre Faribault; Bottom L, 1st Canadian Parachute Battalion; Bottom R, Brenda Beech; 65, Pierre Faribault; 66, Jim Jones; 67, 1st Canadian Parachute Battalion

FOR THOSE IN PERIL ON THE SEA
68–69, George Vant Haaf; 72, Top L, Peter Chance; Top R, John Gorsline; Bottom, Bill MacDonald; 73, John Burgess; 74, Pat Nixon; 75, George Borgal; 76, John Gorsline; 77–79, Tom Ingham; 80–81, Jim Melvin; 82, Forbes Brown; 83, Top, Forbes Brown; Bottom, Pat Nixon; 84, Left, Dusty Lutes; Right, Frank Cauley; 85, Frank Cauley; 86–87, Bill MacDonald; 88, Pat Nixon; 89, Top, Tony Griffin; Bottom L, John Burgess; Bottom R, Peter Stanger; 90, Bill MacDonald; 91, Top, Clarence Brown; Bottom, Peter Chance; 92, E.T. Heathcote; 93, ANA Sidney, BC; 94–97, John Gorsline

DANGEROUS MOONLIGHT
98–99, Merv Couse; 102, Top, Jim Kenny; Bottom L, Dusty Lutes; Bottom R, Marcel Croteau; 103, Doug Appleton; 104, Vern Williams; 105, Top, Alex Gray; Bottom, Wally Loucks; 106, Alex Gray; 107, Top, Alex Gray; Bottom, Art Sager; 108, Bert Coles; 109, Dick Corbett; 110, Marcel Croteau; 111, Bert Coles; 112, Top, Marcel Croteau; Bottom L, Geoff Marlow; Bottom R, Marcel Croteau; 113, Jack Gouinlock; 114–115, Bert Coles; 116, Bert Coles; 117, ANA Sidney, BC; 118, Top, Hugh Godefroy; Bottom L, Hugh Godefroy; Bottom R, Alex Gray; 119, Alex Gray; 120, Merv Couse; 121, Top, Dusty Lutes; Bottom, Merv Couse; 122, Dusty Lutes; 123, Don

Cheney; 124, Top L, Alex Gray; Top R, Vern Williams; Bottom, Bert Coles; 125, Alex Gray; 126, Vern Williams; 127, Don Cheney

THE FACE OF BATTLE

128–129, Geoff Costeloe; 132–133, Bert Coles; 134, Top, Forbes Brown; Bottom, Tony Griffin; 135, Pat Nixon; 136, Geoff Marlow; 137–138, E.T. Heathcote; 139, Top, Nita Walt; Bottom, E.T. Heathcote; 140–141, ANA Sidney, BC; 142, Top L, Laurie Wilmot; Top R, Dick Likely; Bottom, E.T. Heathcote; 143–145, E.T. Heathcote; 146, L & R, John Gorsline; 146–147, Spread, Alex Gray; 148, Top, George Vant Haaf; Bottom L, John Gorsline; Bottom R, E.T. Heathcote; 149, George Vant Haaf; 150–151, Geoff Costeloe; 152–153, 1st Canadian Parachute Battalion; 154, Forbes Brown; 155, Wally Loucks; 156, L, Alex Gray; R, Percy Loosemore; 157, L, Percy Loosemore; R, Geoff Costeloe; 158, Top, Fred Pollak; Bottom L, 1st Canadian Parachute Battalion; Bottom R, Percy Loosemore; 159, Fred Pollak; 160, Top, E.T. Heathcote; Bottom, Alex Gray; 161, Percy Loosemore; 162, E.T. Heathcote; 163, Percy Loosemore

IN FAITHFUL COMPANY

164–165, Bob Mullin; 168, Merv Couse; 169, Bob Dixon; 170, Jean-Claude Dubuc; 171, Top, E.T. Heathcote; Bottom L, Jim Melvin; Bottom R, George Vant Haaf; 172, Top, Percy Loosemore; Bottom, Wally Loucks; 173, Florence Pennington; 174, Top L, Irene Kendrew; Top R, Vern Williams; Bottom, Bert Coles; 175, ANA Sidney, BC; 176, Nora Cook; 177, Top, Bert Coles; Bottom, Anne McNamara; 178, William MacAskill; 179, Ed Haddon; 180, Top L, Jim Campbell; Top R, Vickie LaPrairie; Bottom L, Hugh Godefroy; Bottom R, John Stroud; 181, Dick Likely; 182, Victor Wong; 183, Top, Pat Nixon; Bottom, E.T. Heathcote; 184, Top, Dusty Lutes; Bottom, Bill MacDonald; 185, E.T. Heathcote; 186, Bert Coles; 187, Top, Hugh Godefroy; Bottom, Peter Chance; 188, Top, Alex Jardine; Bottom, Bert Coles; 189, Tony Craven; 190, Top, Peter Briscoe; 2nd from Top, Morden Walker; 3rd from Top, Pierre Faribault; Bottom, Howard McNamara; 191, Top, Dick Field; 2nd from Top, 1st Canadian Parachute Battalion; 3rd from Top, Marcel Croteau; Bottom, John Gorsline; 192, Nora Cook; 193, Bill Jenkins; 194, Tom Ingham; 195, Bert Coles

ACCIDENTAL TOURISTS

196–197, Percy Loosemore; 200 - 201, R.V. Stevenson; 202, Alex Gray; 203, Top, Alex Gray; Bottom, Dick Likely; 204, Top, John Gorsline; 204–205 spread, Nora Cook; 206, Top, Dick Likely; 206, Bottom L, E.T. Heathcote; Bottom R, Vern Williams; 207, William MacAskill; 208, E.T. Heathcote; 209, Percy Loosemore; 210, ANA Sidney,

BC; 211, George Vant Haaf; 212, Bert Coles; 213, Forbes Brown; 214, Bert Coles; 215, Doug Appleton; 216, Dick Likely; 217, Top, Laurie Wilmot; Bottom, Tony Craven; 218, Top, Dick Corbett; Bottom, Bob Dixon; 219, George Vant Haaf; 220, Alex Gray; 221, Percy Loosemore; 222, Top, Alex Gray; Bottom, Percy Loosemore; 223, Top, Dick Likely; Bottom, Dick Field; 225, William MacAskill; 226–227, William MacAskill; 228, Dick Likely; 229, Top, Percy Loosemore; Bottom, Jean-Claude Dubuc; 230, Percy Loosemore; 231, Jean-Claude Dubuc

UNFORGETTABLE AND UNFORGOTTEN

232–233, Archie Byatt; 237, Grant McRae; 238, Ed Haddon; 239, Top, ANA Sidney, BC; Bottom, Percy Loosemore; 240–241, ANA Sidney, BC; 242, Alex Gray; 243, John Gorsline; 244, 1st Canadian Parachute Battalion; 245, Top, Herb Peppard; Bottom, 1st Canadian Parachute Battalion; 246, Roy Pellant; 247, Top, Grant McRae; Bottom, © Australian War Museum*; 248–249, Alex Gray; 250, Top, Dick Likely; Bottom, Bert Coles; 251–252, E.T. Heathcote; 253, Top, Percy Loosemore; Bottom, Alex Gray; 254, Top, Percy Loosemore; Bottom, 1st Canadian Parachute Battalion; 255, Percy Loosemore; 256, Anne McNamara; 257–259, E.T. Heathcote; 260, Top, Leopold Beauchamp; Bottom, Maurice Tugwell; 261, E.T. Heathcote; 262, William MacAskill; 263, Percy Loosemore

MAPLE LEAF UP

264–65, 1st Canadian Parachute Battalion; 268, Top, E.T. Heathcote; Bottom, Irene Kendrew; 269, Doug Appleton; 270–271, Herb Lim; 272, Charles Phelan; 273–274, Dick Likely; 275, E.T. Heathcote; 276, Hugh Godefroy; 277, Vern Williams; 278, Dick Likely; 279–280, E.T. Heathcote; 281, Top, Pat Nixon; Bottom, Forbes Brown; 282, E.T. Heathcote; 283, Jim Jones; 284, Top L, Richard MacFarlane; Top R, Pierre Faribault; Bottom L, E.T. Heathcote; Bottom R, 1st Canadian Parachute Battalion; 285, Richard MacFarlane; 286, Alf Hebbes; 287, 1st Canadian Parachute Battalion; 288, Clem Pearce; 289, Morden Walker; 290, Top, E.T. Heathcote; Bottom, Hilda Ashwell; 291–293, E.T. Heathcote; 294–295, Percy Loosemore; 296, Alex Gray; 297, E.T. Heathcote; 298, Jim Jones; 299, E.T. Heathcote; 300, Top, 1st Canadian Parachute Battalion; Bottom, Percy Loosemore; 301, Jim Jones; 302, Herb Lim; 303, Marcel Croteau; 304, Top, Dick Field; Bottom, Morden Walker; 305, Percy Loosemore; 306, John Acheson; 307, 1st Canadian Parachute Battalion; 308, Nora Cook

COLOPHON

324, E.T. Heathcote

Allied POWs rushing to freedom after a 600-mile journey
from their various camps, Lubeck, Germany, May 1945.

A SOLDIER'S VIEW was

Edited by Martha Kanya-Forstner

Designed by CS Richardson

Typeset, assembled, and coordinated for production by Carla Kean

Printed and bound by Transcontinental Printing

THE ROYAL CANADIAN SCHOOL OF